A BREED APART

Philip Bourjaily

George Bird Evans

Charles Fergus

Steve Grooms

Tom Huggler

Robert E. Jones

Randy Lawrence

Gary Marek

Thomas McIntyre

Geoffrey Norman

Dan O'Brien

Glen Sheppard

Charles Waterman

A BREED APART

A Tribute to the Hunting Dogs that Own Our Souls
An Original Anthology – Volume I

Edited by Doug Truax
Illustrations by Bruce Langton

COUNTRYSPORT PRESS • Traverse City, Michigan

©1993 by Countrysport, Inc.
Illustrations ©1993 by Bruce Langton

First Edition
10 9 8 7 6 5 4 3 2 1

Published by Countrysport Press
P.O. Box 1856, Traverse City, MI 49685

Book and jacket design - Saxon Design, Cedar, Michigan

Printed in the United States of America

Library of Congress Catalog Card Number: 93-073424

ISBN 0-924357-38-X Trade Edition
ISBN 0-924357-40-1 Deluxe Limited Edition

CONTENTS

To Richard A. Wolters
1920–1993

He, too, is here in these pages
and wherever gun dog lovers gather

INTRODUCTION

by Doug Truax

I trained my first bird dog armed, as I often am, with too many books, too many theories, and only the vaguest idea of what I was doing. I was soon convinced by a high-octane English setter puppy and all the vagaries of the grouse woods that this dog training business was less of an exact science than the books had made it out to be. Much less.

But despite frustration, confusion, and occasional moments of sheer chaos, I quickly came to see that hunting birds without a canine companion was not hunting at all. Humans, if they minded their manners and were close friends, were sometimes fun to have along. The dog, however ill-mannered or unruly it might be that day, was *always* welcome.

The high white tail of a setter bounding through the thickets and occasionally, God willing, bounding back in my direction, could illuminate the depressing gray of a November afternoon. I came to live each autumn to see the white form etched, high-headed and motionless, in a weave of saplings, to enter the mysterious scent world that stretched ahead of her nose guided only by her eyes and impossibly taut body, to feel the air explode.

I enjoy the company of other hunters, but I enjoy it most after the hunt, or during the winter and summer months when we recall tales of hunting, which are as often as not tales of dogs and their deeds and misdeeds. The process, I am sure, is like that of support groups for recovering alcoholics or compulsive gamblers, except that hunting dog owners, while they may enjoy consolation and can even tolerate a little mild advice, seldom if ever are willing to take the cure. In fact, the solution to many folks' problems with gun dogs is more of the same. You can't quite keep that raw-boned pointer in the same congressional district you are in, so rather than taking up golf or sending him off to boarding school, you come to the conclusion that another pup might be just the answer. Maybe if you bred ol' Jess into a more sedate line, the new dogs would hunt like oiled machines. The problem, of course, is that most of us will never live long enough to see a happy end to this logic. With gun dogs, most of us are dealt only a few hands in a lifetime; we settle for something less than a royal flush.

Which is why this is such an endlessly fascinating game. In few fields is the Platonic ideal so raggedly approximated by reality. Sporting dogs are sublime when everything falls beautifully into place—abundant game behaving in predictable ways, a skilled hunter, a dog that performs flawlessly. Seldom is it so. So we struggle with imperfection, with dreams that never quite materialize, with promises we can never quite fulfill.

That, of course, makes sporting dogs the perfect material for good story making, and telling. Good writers thrive on ambiguity; great stories get told when there is a need to explain the inexplicable.

So when the opportunity to put together an anthology of original stories on hunting dogs presented itself, I jumped at it with enthusiasm. Here was a chance to gather old writer friends, whether they were ones I've shared the field with or writers whose stories I'd read often enough to think I had, and listen to them spin a yarn or two. The problem was, I confess, that my enthusiasm for gun dogs got the better of me. I ended up with more good stories than would reasonably fit in one volume, so we at Countrysport Press decided to publish them in two volumes over two years.

We made no attempt to structure the book around particular themes or to systematically cover every type of hunting dog. My own prejudice in dogs matches that of Glen Sheppard, whose opinions are never meek—you hunt birds (grouse and woodcock) with a setter, mainly white, and a gun with two barrels. But, hell, a gun dog is a gun dog: a creature to be admired. Some of my most enjoyable days in the field have been behind springers (a fact I am loath to admit to my springer-owning friends) and if I were more of a duck hunter I'd own another golden retriever in a minute. Some of the best dog stories I ever heard were about a bird hunting beagle.

So we went to some of the finest writers we knew working today and simply asked them for the best dog story they had to tell. The writers come from the chukar country of the West to the Green Mountains of Vermont, from the northern grouse woods to the southern quail fields and duck marshes. Here you'll meet some familiar writers whose stories we've all been enjoying for over forty years, and some young writers whose work you may not have yet had a chance to read. Among them are novelists, professional outdoor writers, newspapermen, dog trainers, and writers you may have thought wrote only about big game or fly fishing. But they are all writers, through and through, and they all share a love of the hunting dog. One writer, who breeds and trains pointing dogs, even ended up writing about his horse…and in the process tells us much about dogs.

Each story here, by the way, was written especially for this book. What you'll read is intended for pure enjoyment, although do not be surprised if you find, as I did, that you come away learning more about handling and training a hunting dog than you have through the conventional manuals. I think back to those armfuls of technical books with which I started training my first setter and realize that none of them contained the training medicine I found in these stories. That medicine has nothing to do with electronic collars, whoa commands, or whistle blasts. It has much to do with commitment and defeat, with obsession, acceptance, and even joy.

So pull a chair up close to the fire, sit back, and listen to a talented group of writers discuss one of the most enjoyable, perplexing, and endlessly fascinating subjects I can think of—the hunter and his dog.

George Bird Evans was born with English setters eighty-six years ago and has never been without them. He had to be away from them while studying art, and then in New York working toward being an illustrator, and arriving, but even then there were the grouse seasons with his father and the setters in southwest Pennsylvania. Kay was introduced to Speck as seriously as to George's parents, and until 1935 Speck was with George and Kay whenever they could be at the mountain cabin. In 1939 they realized their own place in the Alleghenies, named it Old Hemlock, and bought Blue, the beginning of their Old Hemlock line. His son Ruff pointed and retrieved grouse from 1947 to 1962, sired three litters, and saw George put away paint brushes and start writing. Twenty-two books and many anthology and magazine pieces later, Quest and his son, eleventh-generation Manton, now live and hunt with George and Kay, who could not exist without a setter.

BITTERSWEET

by George Bird Evans

Without the alchemy of Indian summer the shooting man would have only gray days from August to December, deprived of hazy afternoons and the war paint of the mountains; no glow of sugar maples progressing into flame, no newly minted aspen copse atremble in soft winds, no wincing yearning for days and moments like lemon-yellow leaves coming down counting Time that won't come back; no fermentation stirring primordial memory, no pungency of October's rot, no expectation. None of those smells and agonies and visions would be here to make it good, to make us go on living it after it has passed, remembering, wanting, hungering for it to come again.

It had come again and we were driving out our long lane with black lace of hemlocks a fairyland against sugar-maple gold, and I felt somehow that everything was going to be like the old days. Belton and Quest peering out the tailgate window seemed to know it was the week of the season when generations of Old Hemlock setters from Ruff through Dixie and Bliss and Briar had come under the spell of the big woodcock coverts of the Blackwater/Canaan, and we were off.

Partway to the Valley, Kay turned the station wagon into a side road and up a hill leading to high coverts that had to hold flight woodcock this last week of October. Winding up the dirt road doubling back on itself, we could look down through gnarled apple trees to the empty unpainted house where the old man, gray as the clapboards, used to wave to us where now his makeshift ladder still leaned against the roof.

We topped the last bend through vines blue with wild grapes, and leveled along the straight stretch with all things beautiful until we came to the yellow No Hunting notices plastering our first covert. We drove on with them glaring at us for half a mile, even at the Poplar House where the entrance had been plowed into a hostile barrier with one more yellow rectangle nailed on the wooden gate.

Farther down the hill we parked with the station wagon canted on the side of the rough road. I at least had a permit marked "lifetime" in my shooting vest that said I could hunt here.

While I was changing into rubber pacs a car labored up the stony grade and stopped and a white-haired man in a Stewart tartan shirt—why do some old men look like some old women—inquired if I wasn't Mr. Evans. There was a patient-looking woman on the seat beside him instead of a dog and she listened quietly while he told me he was from the southern part of the state. It seemed a West Virginia game biologist had said he could find woodcock in here, and had marked his map *George Bird Evans's cover*. I thought of Col. Peter Hawker's *Diary* and

"that green-livered son of a bitch, the lawyer." He finally left, after telling me there weren't any birds in there.

We cast Belton and Quest and they leaped the sagging wire fence and began quartering through leaves too dry and noisy. The old man had been right: we didn't move a feather all the way to the hemlock swamp in the bottom. Crossing back over the road, I was certain we'd find 'cock among the hillside hawthorns but both dogs covered them well and there was nothing, not even in Belton's rail fence corner.

Waiting for Kay, who had gone for the station wagon, I sat on the top rail with memories of the birds in Belton's younger days and tried to make some sense out of it. Today was cool, forty-five degrees, and partly sunny, and it was the last day of October, when my setters and I had so many times been mesmerized by flighting woodcock in this sleepy Rip Van Winkle hollow. This season there were no cattle grazing around the Poplar House, but could woodcock anticipate that and bypass a covert such as this? The charm of the old road was beginning to work its hypnosis when Kay pulled the station wagon to a stop and brought me out of my reverie.

At the bottom of the hill we crossed the stream and let the dogs out. There was a barbed wire fence and we took turns spreading the strands for the other to squeeze through. There were cow pads—big, juicy, lovely—and a hen woodcock came back over us fast and sassy and was gone.

Here in the open lowland it was windy and colder and we worked cattle paths through the red-berried hawthorns. Out ahead I saw Quest on point in a dense spinney below a small shed. This was what I had waited for all summer, with daily therapeutic drymounting the new little 28-bore AyA. Ten days ago there had been a reinjury of the right shoulder, bringing back the old pain, but now it was going to be all right. I couldn't see Belton, but Quest was holding—a high-headed angel, his bloody tail tip vivid in the sunshine. A woodcock, another hen, gave me everything in a rising straightaway over the spiky thicket and my shoulder atrophied with the gunstock partway out from under my arm. Some things are more bitter than pain.

We hunted higher into good cover, stepping around more cow pads, but had no reflush. On top we came to what from a distance had appeared to be out-of-scale sheep—off-white Charolais, lots of them. Quest had a point that proved empty and Belton, the rascal, wouldn't honor—*there was no bird, was there?*

Just before we left home I had discovered a suspicious swelling on Belton. He was approaching thirteen and in apparent good health, but our vet had sent off a specimen for biopsy. With a week to wait for the report, we had come on this trip as the best way to get through the uncertainty until diagnosis, and I was grateful for any pleasure Belton had.

Quest gave us another point, a hot one, but the flush wouldn't have been a shot, even with a good shoulder. It was nearing end of day when we reached the station wagon, and Kay put Belton into the rear and stayed with him while I took one more turn with Quest in search of the first 'cock that had flushed to the north side of the road.

The thicket was too dense to penetrate, but I heard Quest's bell go silent. I made a short circle into swamp grass on the outside, and then the bell spoke again, and the woodcock came out against the sunset and bloomed into vision, whizzing past me. I wheeled and tried to mount and again the shoulder just wouldn't do it. The stock felt a foot too long, and I was still subconsciously trying to start the mount by the Churchill method, high up under the arm against the ribs. You can't unlearn years of habit in a day.

It was well after dark when we reached our rented Canaan Valley cabin, but we were soon set up with Belton and Quest fed and spread out on their blanket on the sofa. This was the end of October, the flights would logically be in; if Belton's report proved negative, it would seem we just about had everything.

Next day was cloudy and sunny by turns with a wind that made the forty-seven degree temperature seem cold. We parked inside a rickety iron gate leading to a huge pasture grown to copses of hawthorns and red maples, with a draw of spruce and fir and alders tapering into tundra.

There was a rutted trace of road and Belton and Quest went on point at the very cluster of thicket where they'd had a point last season. As I circled in front, a woodcock flushed head high and to my delight I got the gun up and fired. I felt I might have hit but Quest bored out, and although we got both dogs back to search carefully they found neither bird nor feathers. To a man for whom a shot like that would normally have almost certainly been a hit, such misses are devastating.

With Belton and Quest wild with excitement, we hunted south into alders bordering the balsam swamp. I remember Bliss pointing there on a day when she and Dixie were in their prime, with Bliss's tail straight up; I also remember that I missed the 'cock, and there was nothing wrong with my shoulder then.

On Quest's next point with Belton backing, a woodcock went up before I reached the dogs, and soon after, Quest had another productive in the edge cover. Woodcock may not like to get their feet wet, as I am told, but there was whitewash floating in a small puddle. I splashed to Quest, who was rigid, then took two more steps and heard a bell-like twitter-up behind me and wheeled and fired at a silhouette topping the alders. The muscle spasm threw the pattern to the right and I watched the 'cock disappear, dropping a departing token. Old Alaric Alexander Watts advised: "try to draw the trigger just as you at the gun's end the object view. Nine times in ten the gun is right. ..." I was having too many tens, and becoming a little vocal about it, then recalled Nash Buckingham at ninety, gamely trying to shoot with vision in only one eye.

We had come to an area new to us, with tundra sweeping into the south and alders delineating a tiny run, which was widening into a series of beaver dams, with blue Cabin Mountain scalloping the sky to the east. We reached a low rise with a view of hawthorns ahead of us and stopped to eat lunch sitting on an outcrop of rock under two of the larger trees. Unlike the hawthorns we hunted yesterday, these spiky branches held no haws where there would normally have been red or yellow globes, but woodcock would be there for the leaf-pack on the ground, not the fruit.

It was sunny on this big plain, with huge cumulus repeated in shadow on Cabin Mountain. Kay got some pictures of Belton seriously watching her for the biscuit he knew she would have brought him, and here in this glorious land it seemed he just had to be all right.

Starting after lunch both dogs reached out—Belton as far as Quest—but on our way north we felt he needed resting, and Kay led him on leash while Quest and I skirted tall woods with excellent thorns. When we came to the far end Kay released Belton, who hadn't taken his eyes off me, and he worked the damp leaf-pack under the big hawthorns with Quest. There were almost always 'cock in here and Belton soon gave us a nice point that Quest honored loyally. Woodcock were nervous this season, going up like killdeer. There were two birds, one a climbing flush I would normally have tried for, but my clumsy misses on this trip had robbed me of my confidence and I didn't take the shot. That was the end of the action. Regrettably I gave Belton and Quest nothing to retrieve but Quest made do with a couple of deer legs he delivered to me religiously, souvenirs of the bow hunting that goes on throughout the bird season in the Canaan.

In the night it began to snow and we awoke to a white Canaan Valley with Cabin and Canaan mountains fogged out in the upper elevations. By late morning it was up to fifty-five degrees with a flawless sky but still breezy. We had saved one big covert in the upper Valley for such a day as this, a place we discovered only the previous season.

Taking time to pack for the drive home after the hunt, it was past 1:00 p.m. when we cast Belton and Quest. The area was an expanse of flatland dotted with hawthorns—big as hawthorns are big in this strange highland. Quest was moving wide, fitting himself to the scale of the covert but Belton found the first woodcock in a corner nearby, a bird that bored out like a bullet.

It has been my experience that 'cock act differently in open situations, refusing to hold for the gun, and I wondered if it was the lack of overhead cover or pressure from recent gunners making them spooky. When I first came to the Canaan, one of the regulars, a shooting M.D. who reserved a room throughout the season at the old Worden's Hotel in Davis, used to say: "There is no such thing as a private covert in this Blackwater country," and it is true. Curiously, you don't always see the other hunters, but I can tell by the action of my dogs and sometimes by the behavior of the birds when other gunners and their dogs have been there.

Wind was at our backs, seeming to gain velocity out in the bottom, and although Quest was trying to work with it in his face, he ran onto a woodcock in a small copse of hawthorns and stopped conscientiously at the flush, the strong breeze ruffling the hair the wrong way on his back. He stood watching the bird disappear, followed by another and another, until five 'cock had lifted from the one thicket, flushing in as many directions. One crossed up the slope in front of me, a nice chance that I passed—I don't shoot at woodcock unless they're pointed—and Quest moved on, trying to avoid my look.

There were so many points and wild flushes that counting separate woodcock was difficult. Belton hunted hard, even ranging too wide but keeping in touch, while Quest, stimulated by so much action, had to be checked at times.

We made a big circle, and at the south-end woods ate sandwiches as we sat on twin stumps. Quest had pointed a 'cock at the head of the little draw and Kay had got some pictures; now she took more of our blue/orange brace resting.

Starting out after lunch we almost immediately had a double point among small hawthorns—a male bird that came out low-crossing right, a shot I tried too close and missed and missed again as it banked, but it is odd that two empty shots can be an event to a man with atrophied shoulders, and I rejoiced that I shot at all. I recalled how I used to handle my $7\,^3/_4$-pound Fox in dense grouse cover, and I can still see 'cock folding in puffs of tan feathers when I was using the little Purdey—split-second shots in dense alders and spiraea jungles.

Quest had another point breathing fire—a hen looking larger than hens look and right-quartering through the orchard-size hawthorns. My mount was so cramped I shot from my right biceps and the bird looked as if it had no intention of ever stopping.

In our three days of gunning we had been in more hawthorns than I can remember anywhere, with almost no aspens, which normally spell woodcock to me, but the 'cock were there.

By this time Quest was pointing again in dead goldenrod beyond the station wagon. I got to him and stepped past and the woodcock darted for the edge of beech woods. I like to think I might have dropped it *if,* but Quest made a dash in my line of fire, high on adrenaline from seeing too many birds fly on unhit. Lady Luck is a fickle hussy, irresistible and charming, and there was a time when she and I were on more intimate terms.

I had an urge to continue, but Belton was showing signs of tiring, and I knew, without facing it too squarely, that I was not going to make any shots with my humerus and acromion grinding bone-on-bone each time I mounted my gun. The little 28-bore was a delight to carry and the 2 dram $^3/_4$ ounce #9 loads were pleasant to shoot, but merely hearing them go off was not what I came for.

Changing out of my boots, we headed the station wagon up Canaan Mountain, pausing at the top to look back down on the wild spread of aspen and spruce bogs with the Blackwater winding from one beaver dam to the next, each a piece of misplaced evening sky. It was a land Robert W. Service wrote about without ever having seen it: *I am the land that listens, I am the land that broods.* ... Behind me I could hear Quest licking his wet coat and Belton trying to find a comfortable position for his tired bones. We drove homeward toward Old Hemlock with the old gibbous Woodcock Moon changing from right to left and back again as we unwound the narrow curving road.

On Monday we got the report on Belton's biopsy. But we had given him three more wonderful days.

Charles F. Waterman says he quit honest work shortly after World War II and has been a freelance outdoor writer for nearly fifty years. Before that war he was a newspaper writer and photographer and during it he skippered a Steichen combat photo team with the Navy in the Pacific. He was raised on a Kansas farm, wrote his first outdoor column in 1934, and has written seventeen hunting and fishing books, some of which, he says, disappeared without a ripple. He says that at one point when he and his wife Debie were faced with starvation he taught literature for a year at Stetson University. Their home is in Florida but for more than thirty years they have spent summer and part of the fall in Montana.

POINTING WEST

by Charles F. Waterman

These western pointing dogs generally have a special look, as if they know things ordinary field trial champions and woodcock wizards haven't heard of. It is a secretive, conniving look that comes from listening for the soft cackle of chukars from distant rimrock and catching the rising scent of sage hens from far down the deep draws, with pronghorns watching from the ridges.

The man at the door had a sleek little pointer under his arm and she did not have the Wild West look. She was confused.

"This is a wonderful little dog," he said. "She came from back East and she has great papers, but she won't point Huns or sharptails and she looks funny when they fly."

I know all about that business.

"Just give her time," I said. "Come in and have some coffee."

The little pointer performed well before the Hun season was over, and for years she ran the canyon edges for chukars, grinned craftily at the aspen patches where the ruffed grouse lived, and watched the flight of wild-flushing western pheasants she hoped to catch up to when they had found a tight coulee. But I had made an educated guess. Not all pointing dogs can adapt to enormous stubble fields and the brush-choked foothill creek bottoms. For that matter, there are prosperous corporation lawyers who might not excel in defending the winner of a barroom fight.

I have a special qualification in the western dog business, even though I am a poor dog trainer and gave away a big-time field trial winner because I couldn't see his potential. My qualification is that in a goofy, self-imposed project I once shot all of the species of pointable North American upland birds over a single Brittany named Kelly. Although he was never really steady to wing and shot, he came through the list with a superior attitude toward other dogs and the aforementioned conniving look when the dog box opened. Now the project took no particular skill on my part, but I have found that mentioning it in the beginning of any dog tirade such as this gives me a protective pad of authenticity. My friends—and possibly my few scattered readers—are sick and tired of hearing of it. But some dog experts have never shot ptarmigan on Alaska's Donnelly's Dome or Mearns quail on the Mexican border. See?

There are western traditions concerning horses, hats, and boots, but somehow, the list of upland birds has been left out, possibly because prairie chickens seemed trivial when they lived near elk and grizzly bears. Only a few years back, it was hard to buy much of anything but duck and goose loads in the smaller sporting good stores and youngsters thought "Full Choke" was part of a shotgun's trade name. That was when Huns were "little chickens" or "quail" and the rancher said there were no real grouse (meaning blues) on the mountain, although there were some of those little "ruffled grouse" down in the creek bottoms.

But even then there were specialists like Mac (a Brittany named for the trout fly, Rat-faced MacDougall), who followed ruffed grouse pedestrians into the willows and thatched brush along ice-edged little trout streams. When the grouse fluttered up

into low limbs to inspect and cluck at the strangely spotted coyote, Mac would climb the tree after it with gutteral canine profanity. If you could get down in there without breaking a leg you might get an impossible shot at the disgusted bird as it bored off through the branches.

A Pennsylvania grouse lover observed Mac's procedure with distaste and explained to me that it was a different species of bird from the king of eastern coverts. I agreed, saving his day, although ardent study of grouse biology had shown the birds in the deep-cut creek bottoms were clinically indistinguishable from their more refined relatives.

For years there was the Big Field—an enormous flat of wheatgrass, some three miles across and with the ever-present backdrop of a great mountain, generally white on top. It was many miles to the mountain but it seemed to begin at the edge of the field where it began to break into draws and benches. Perhaps the Big Field was a bench itself, as it seemed a part of the big mountain.

Below the field on the side opposite the mountain was a pattern of steep-sided sage brush draws, leading down to more flats and more draws that led down to creeks that fed a river miles away. When I first saw the Big Field I put a big rawboned English pointer down from the truck and watched her catch the wind and fly—for once with all the running room she wanted. For a moment I had the familiar helpless feeling of watching a dog seemingly out of control, but I watched her bend a cast more sharply and turn to a high-tailed point at the head of one of the sage arroyos.

I hurried and panted and muttered instructions that the dog could not possibly hear, and when I came alongside her, shaky and panting, the covey of sharptail grouse went up with their monotonal "cuk, cuk, cuk" to swing down the sage-lined arroyo. I atoned for a shaky miss to get one bird. She was a young pointer then, and it was years later when she pointed her last birds at the head of the draw—Hungarian partridge that time. In other years she had found burly sage grouse there—a natural exit from sage to grass.

It must have been in places like the Big Field that big-going pointing dogs were developed. The pointer who found those first birds at the tip of the coulee rejoiced in those square miles of open grass and would be a streaking white speck so far away there was no place for the word "control." I and any companion I might have would trudge along with our eyes watering a little from strain and wind and watch the speeding speck with its backdrop of snowy mountain. Now I am sure we must have faced the other way much of the time but I always think of Duchess before the mountain. Her full name was Duchess of Doonesbury.

When the white speck stopped we took deep breaths and started toward her, walking at flank speed, and grumbling when we saw our white marker move again to stop once more, for birds of the wide open will walk and run, and only the right dog can follow them at the proper distance and keep them on the ground.

So when we came close to Dutch we'd come up alongside her, getting an impatient glance from an eye that moved slightly sidewise in an unmoving head, and we would walk forward with her as she cat-footed in starts and stops, altering direction slightly as the unseen birds changed course. It would be Huns, sharptails, or sage grouse, and when they finally flew I always wanted to shoot too soon, before I was really on. Such pointing tactics are not followed by trial winners but it was Dutch's field and she ran the show.

When Spike, the engaging, leggy Brittany, appeared in our kennel, he accepted Dutch as the Big Field autocrat that she was, and although he could cast almost as widely as she did, he willingly gave up his points to her. In other covers Dutch might be as polite as a self-centered sixty-two-pound barn burner could be, but when the dog box opened and she hit the ground in *her* field, lesser individuals were only assistants at best. If Spike found birds and pointed, Dutch might turn away as if assuming he had a meadow-lark or, if the scent was strong, she would simply soft-foot ahead of him and assume her dramatic pointing stance, which implied the entire world was about to erupt in squawks and feathers.

Once, when a covey of Huns seemed to be zigzagging up ahead, Spike happened to maneuver so that he was nearest to them, a situation Dutch evidently considered the matter of a child doing an adult's work. In silence, except for the soft thumps of her feet on the ground and the whip of wheatgrass about her legs, she charged the unsuspecting Spike, striking him just back of the shoulders with her broad chest, and he was knocked into kicking impotence while Dutch assumed her postcard pointing stance. Instead of showing rage or surprise, Spike simply rolled to his feet, took a backing position, and appeared apologetic. Sorry about that.

When I recall sage grouse, I think of the giant world they live in, the occasional pickup trails that may once have been wagon trails, the coyote shadow I am not quite sure I saw, and the sky with wind-torn clouds the way Charlie Russell painted them. I think too of old Tex, the big-shouldered Brittany, who was never quite convinced that sage hens should be handled as other birds. I think Tex had given them considerable thought while catching shreds of scent at the heads of sage-filled coulees and believed that with the right approach an enterprising bird dog could catch one.

Tex, who had impeccable ancestry along with the paper name of Tip Top Texican, was simply a burly Brittany who over-stepped the Brittany specifications a little when it came to fighting weight. Willing to do a perfect job of pointing a scattered covey of five-pound sage hens after soft-footing upwind for hundreds of yards, Tex felt that fulfilled his obligation to me. But after the first bird was in the air and I was groping for it with a shotgun, Tex would try to catch the rest. Sage grouse are often a bit scattered and there are numerous sleepers, each of which Tex would charge with abandon. I always thought he wanted to bark at them but felt it was beneath his dignity. He maintained more decorum with other plains birds and even did fairly well on ruffed grouse in late fall aspen patches.

I have heard that pointing dogs cannot work well in sage because it kills their scenting abilities, an observation on the same level as the report that gunpowder in their food makes them run faster. I once said that I felt a flock of sage hens probably put out roughly the same amount of scent as a battalion of infantry after a week's maneuvers. I love to see a canny old western campaigner catch the scent of sage hens, especially when he's at the high end of a draw and the air is rising. He quarters cautiously and gradually begins to narrow his beat until he begins to roll his eyes in anticipation and I check the location of the safety repeatedly and keep telling myself that if I get a couple of shots I should reload quickly for the sleepers.

But sometimes sage hens run. Well, maybe we should call it "power walking," as the physical education experts say. A sage grouse takes pretty big steps and there are times when it appears as a moving dark spot on a distant slope since it is the color of sage and only its dark shadow gives it away. A birdy dog once stuck to a long sage hen trail followed by my friend with a Model 12 Winchester and by me with a truck. The trail was a mile long and only one bird put up out of range. We knew it had been a covey but the other birds had peeled off and the dog had to make a choice. In that mile he had pointed many times but sensed his targets were moving on. I don't know how many decisions he had to make as his covey melted away on both sides.

But while field trial judges shake their heads and squirm in their saddles, it must be said that many of the Wild West birds do not play the game quite fairly, and although "Gentleman Bob" is a common term for bobwhite quail, I have never heard of a gentleman sage grouse. In dealing with such game it is necessary to abandon some of the procedures that work smoothly for birds that hold tightly and fly hard when you wave a thirty dollar flushing whip over them.

So some of the dog work becomes trailing and one visitor asked me why a pair of setters didn't bay like coon hounds since they seemed engaged in long-distance tracking. In truth, the point-and-move program is not classic but is pretty exciting stuff and at least once it ended very strangely. A male Brittany named Kelly was involved, called that simply because the name Murphy had already been put to use, and at the time I was sticking to Irish nomenclature.

Kelly caught the scent and went birdy high on a slope that plunged steeply downward into a little network of draws that carried wet-weather creeks. Kelly was a dramatist who could approach a single bird as if the world had momentarily stopped turning, and after viewing his histrionics for a hundred yards or so veteran gunners have been known to fire wildly into the air when the bird finally flew. In this case I followed him through scraggly sage bushes and past some barren erosions. Some of the dry cuts were several feet deep and only a yard or so wide. Bad washes, as ranchers say.

Finally, Kelly pointed and gave me his look that always said,"Man, they're here and you better be ready!"

So I limped forward, trying to keep my left foot ahead of my right, a very difficult bit of gymnastics, but I figured you could never be too ready, even for big birds that take gravity very seriously and don't get up to flank speed for the first thirty yards. No birds flew and I noted that one of those deep and narrow ditches was immediately ahead of me. In preparing to jump it, I looked down and noted a flock of sage hens wedged into the narrow bottom of the ditch and looking up at me with resignation. They had no room to spread their wings so they had no way to fly out of the ditch, and whoever was in charge of that bunch had really blown it.

Now I may be as bloodthirsty as the next shotgunner, but I am not an executioner and fair is fair, so I turned and walked away, dragging a disgusted Kelly with me. To this day, long since, I wish I had simply retired a few yards and watched all those sage turkeys climb out of that ditch. I wonder if they flew when they had climbed out or if they just walked away with their heads down. Kelly didn't hunt very well the rest of that afternoon and several times I found him watching me with a mixture of disapproval and pity. After all these years he had cornered a covey of birds I could catch with a landing net and I had walked away from them.

I am unhappy to see chukars behaving on game preserves like ordinary birds. Chukars are supposed to be up there where the sage thins out a little and there are long strips of rimrock and great flat boulders that once were rimrock and have crumbled down through the ages. In India, they use chukars as fighting cocks, domesticate them, and carry them around in wicker baskets, according to an authority on the subject. I don't like that either. I want wild chukars where they are hard to get at and I want chukar dogs who listen to their ventriloquistic calls and help me get above them so they'll fly when they're pointed.

I do not believe you train dogs to be chukar experts. It is something that grows in the backs of their scheming minds. Kelly, who regarded bobwhite whistles the same as he regarded meadowlark calls or distant auto horns, would prick his ears and roll his eyes at the first wisp of wind-blown cackle from up there somewhere in any one of the several chukar states. Chukar mountains are not tourist mountains. They are tired, ragged old mountains that go with desert and near-desert lands and often they are above valley quail and their relatives, who sometimes live in the creek bottoms. They have interfered badly with my quail hunting. I took my friend quail hunting, preparing him with glowing terms about Kelly's quail expertise. Let us put in here that you should beware of anyone who promises specific things from a dog. You are consorting with a fool.

It was a brushy Idaho creek and the quail lived there all right. We began moving upstream along the bottom and Kelly worked diligently. He pointed once and the birds moved on him, but the next time he held them and my friend killed a bird that skirted the heavy brush.

It was shortly after that when Kelly stopped on the high side of the creek brush, stood stock still for several seconds, and cocked his head toward the steep slope with its scattered boulders, cheat grass, and shabby little sage bushes. It was not long after that when I could no longer hear his bell and I told my friend to get ready because we had birds ahead. We found nothing and I apprehensively forced myself to stare up the mountainside. Far up there was a little brindle spot moving cautiously among the boulders.

And then I caught a problem sound, coming with a little twist of breeze. It was the chukars' muted cackle from up where Kelly was moving. I got up there and brought him back to the quail hunt, but after he was out of sight ahead of us he went back to the mountain. Once a chukar dog, always a chukar dog. Kelly could not understand why we fooled with the quail. My friend suggested we go in. He said chasing chukars was too much work.

Mike was apparently the result of philandering by a male setter and a Brittany dam, and it is a little vague as to how we came to acquire him. My associate in bird dog matters was always reluctant to compliment "Iron Mike" on his hunting qualities but often said old Mike could whip anything short of a pit bull. This came, from an early career as an alley dog and garbage barrel connoisseur, which occurred before we recognized Mike for his sterling stubble-field qualities and attached him to our little string. Mike could find Huns in stubble fields, and the bigger the stubble field the greater his enthusiasm. He'd hold them until dark.

But Mike had never hunted chukars and his hard driving style seemed like a natural so I took him to Nevada, where I heard chukars calling along a great strip of rimrock, high above a valley jeep trail. It was a long way up but there were a lot of chukars so I started climbing, forcibly holding Mike alongside as much as possible. It was much later that I reached the rimrock objective, loaded my scarred chukar gun, and mentioned to Mike that he could go on and hunt.

It developed that Mike felt chukars were to be caught and not pointed so he ran up a quarter mile of them. I saw them as specks that shot out from the rocks and dived into the valley. Then Mike came back, grinning and lolling his tongue, and evidently feeling he had accomplished the mission. He spent the rest of his chukar career in a dog box.

If the sage hen presents a scent that fills a brushy coulee, the Mearns quail is the opposite, and there was the Mearns veteran who told me to sniff a Gambel's quail and then a Mearns. It's true that with my nose an inch from the Gambel's I really could smell something but I smelled nothing when I tried the Mearns bird— an explanation of why good Mearns dogs often perform as if hunting mice.

I took old hard-charging Dutch to Arizona Mearns country on the Mexican border and put her in perfect cover—little draws that sloped up from a really wide one, and there were the scrub oaks that have been everywhere I've seen Mearns quail. She found birds, her broad snout inches from the ground and her eyes big with the realization she was almost on top of game. I was sure then that my adaptable old friend was a super Mearns dog but an hour later Dutch decided this close-order drill was foolishness and started chasing quail. I took her back to her beloved Huns, sharptails, prairie chicken, and sage grouse.

Let me tell you some time about bird dogs and ptarmigan.

Robert F. Jones was for many years a senior writer at Time and Sports Illustrated. *His essays and short stories have appeared in thirteen previous anthologies and a host of magazines, including* Audubon, Gray's Sporting Journal, *and* Fly Rod & Reel. *He writes a bird-hunting column, "The Dawn Patrol," for* Shooting Sportsman. *Born in Wisconsin, where he learned his love of the outdoors, Jones has since hunted or fished on every continent but Antarctica. The author of five novels and three works of nonfiction, including the award-winning* Upland Passage: A Field Dog's Education, *and* Jake: A Labrador Puppy at Work & Play *(Farrar, Straus & Giroux, 1992), Jones recently completed a sixth novel,* Tie My Bones to Her Back, *set on the Great Plains in the 1870s. A collection of his African hunting tales,* The Heart is One, *will be published next fall by Safari Press.*

RUSTY AND BELLE

by Robert F. Jones

A boy's father should teach him to hunt.

Mine liked to fish. He didn't care much for what they call the shooting sports, and my only hunting uncle happened to be in jail during my formative years. (That's another story.) So my education as a budding Nimrod took a different course. In fact, like Mowgli in Kipling's *Jungle Book*, I was taught how to hunt by the wolves.

Well, okay… so maybe they weren't wolves. But a pair of half-wild, hell-for-leather Irish setters is probably the next best thing.

How Rusty and Belle sniffed me out as a candidate for on-the-job training, I really don't know. I don't even know who actually owned them. And yet, during a single glorious, murderous, never-to-be-forgotten autumn just after World War II, I found myself hunting behind them, gradually learning the nuances of the chase, gunning my first game birds over them, and developing under their rude tutelage a lifelong love of upland shooting. First times, as they say, are always the best.

Ever since my family had moved, in the fall of 1941, to the far western reaches of Wauwatosa in southern Wisconsin, I'd been mesmerized by game birds. Across the road from our newly built home lay a broad belt of virgin tallgrass prairie, stretching nearly a mile down to the Menomonee River. That reach of the upper Middle West is part of what scientists call the Prairie Peninsula, islands of grassland studded across the great, dark-green sea of the northern forests. This configuration provides lots of "edge," and the region was therefore rich in wildlife. Bison had roamed those prairie islands, as far east as Pennsylvania and New York, but the last of Wisconsin's buffalo was killed in 1832. Game birds remained abundant, though. Ruffed grouse, sharptails and prairie chickens, woodcock and snipe, clouds of ducks, and later the newly introduced ringneck pheasant—all proliferated on or around these grassy islands. In those parts, it was almost inevitable that a boy should become an upland hunter.

· · · · ·

That first winter in the new house I began noticing clusters of large, brown, football-shaped birds scuttling around in the field across the road as they fed in the snow on grass seed knocked down by the wind. I was not yet seven years old, but something ignited in my heart. I wanted to hold one in my hands, maybe study its feathers up close, perhaps even pluck them out—though I knew the bird would have to be dead for me to do that. Okay, so I'd kill it first. And then when it was plucked…

And then what?

I'd eat it!

Yes, hunting is instinctive with us, despite the arguments of the antis. *I had to have one of those birds.*

"What are they, Dad?" I asked one afternoon as my father and I were shoveling snow in front of the house. He looked across the street. A dozen of the big birds were feeding busily in the field near the road.

"Prairie chickens," he said.

I stared longingly at them, less than a hundred feet away.

"They don't make good pets," he said.

"I don't want one as a pet," I said. "I want to kill one. We could cook it up for supper tonight."

He laughed.

"Don't let your mother hear you say that," he said. My mother was a notorious critter-lover, weeping quietly whenever a songbird snuffed itself against a storm window, or at the mere thought of a dead raccoon on the road.

One of the birds was feeding toward us, well away from the rest of the flock. "See if you can hit him with a snowball," my dad said.

I packed a good one, as small and heavy and tight and round as I could make it. I crossed the road directly toward the bird. Not even looking up, it scurried back to the flock. I kept going. With every step I gained on them, they edged away deeper into the wind-bent grass. I couldn't get within range this way. I sprinted toward them in nightmare slow motion, the metal clasps of my heavy galoshes rattling as I ran. They scuttled a bit faster. Finally, panting, I hurled the snowball. They avoided it with ease and kept on feeding. By the time I had had enough, I was a quarter of a mile into the prairie, knee-deep in snow, redfaced and slick with sweat, and my arm ached from futile throws at unhittable targets. I plodded back to my father, who was gentleman enough to hide the grin that was threatening to erupt into a boy-shattering guffaw.

"A snowball's no good," I said.

"Guess not."

"Dad, could I have a bow and some arrows?"

"We'll see," he said.

For Christmas that year I received a lemonwood longbow of fifteen pounds pull. I was a big kid for my age, but the bow was too strong for me at first. I persevered, shooting at snowmen in the backyard during the winter, or hay bales or bushel baskets or (when the grownups weren't looking) at the occasional pumpkin in the neighborhood's communal Victory Garden across the road the following summer, and by fall I felt I was ready. I wasn't. Oh, sure, I could shoot a Pound Sweet apple out of the neighbor's backyard tree, and once I grazed a fat robin tugging a worm from the earth after a rainstorm, but I couldn't hit a prairie chicken that first autumn to save my wretched soul. I lost arrow after arrow, shooting at birds on the ground, and never nicked a one. They dodged the arrows as readily as they had my first snowball, and the arrow inevitably slithered off beneath the matted grass, rarely to fly again.

I began making my own arrows out of the long pinewood rods my mom used to support leggy garden plants, fletching them with brightly dyed turkey feathers from a cheap Indian war bonnet that one of my aunts had given me for my eighth birthday. In hopes of saving arrows, I arrived independently at the principle of the flu-flu, in which the fletching is glued around the tail of the shaft in corkscrew fashion to slow down the final flight of the arrow, and learned how to stalk quite close to the flock before shooting—sometimes as close as thirty feet.

Finally I hit a prairie chicken, a young one, just as the flock was rising in panic from my best stalk ever. I broke her wing, and it took me half an hour of frantic chasing through tangles of the low-lying sawgrass we called "ripgut" before I finally batted her flat with the bow. I fell on her like a fumbled football and wrung her rubbery neck.

I sat there in the prairie, with the bluestem towering over my head, my hands and bare forearms stinging from sweat and innumerable grass cuts, with hard, sharp grass seeds stuck in the blood that seeped from the slashes, holding her at last in my hands. She was hot, dusty smelling, heavy, limp, and dead as a doornail. I ruffled the transverse chocolate and white bars on her breast again and again, as I later would the short, thick, soft hair of the first girl I ever loved. Never in my life had I been happier than I was at that moment.

But I knew there had to be a better way.

That way was with a dog and a gun.

· · · · ·

My grandfather, Frank Jones, had led a peripatetic life as a young man, before the turn of the twentieth century. Born in 1871, he'd run away from home in Chicago at the age of fourteen after smashing a slate over a schoolmaster's head when that man falsely accused him of whispering to a classmate. He'd bummed around the Midwest, working on farms, becoming a dab hand with horse teams. He drifted into the small town occasionally, working as a shop clerk, a hackney driver, once as an assistant to an undertaker, among other odd jobs, but finally fetching up back in Chicago. There he became a foreman on the production line in a packing house. The company he worked for, maybe it was Swift or Armour, I can't remember, had developed a revolutionary new canning process, and a New York City packer pirated him away to steal the new technique. He went to New York in 1890 and remained there for nearly ten years. When his boss at the packing plant told him that all employees would be expected to vote for the Republican incumbent, Benjamin Harrison, over Grover Cleveland in the upcoming 1892 presidential election, my grandfather quit his job, though he was still a few months shy of twenty-one and couldn't have voted if he'd wanted to. He was damned if anyone would tell him how to vote.

Out of work, he and an unemployed partner pooled their resources, bought an old 12-bore W.W. Greener hammer gun, rented a team and a buckboard, and went across the Hudson River to the Jersey Palisades to hunt for the New York restaurant market. They brought along a stray dog they'd befriended, a lop-eared, curly coated, liver-colored pooch named Fred who may have been an American water spaniel.

"I didn't care what breed he was," my grandfather used to say. "Old Fred was good at his job and that's all I cared about."

"What did you hunt for?" I asked him.

"Bog-suckers, pa'tridges, and prairie hens," he told me. I later deciphered those names to mean woodcock, ruffed grouse, and—of all things—heath hens, the last-named being the eastern equivalent of my beloved Greater Prairie Chicken (*Tympanuchus cupido*). The heath hen died out in the early years of this century, of course, almost simultaneously with the last of the passenger pigeons which once darkened the skies of nineteenth-century America during their spring and fall migrations, both birds the victims of unbridled habitat destruction and wanton American blood lust.

But while it lasted the hunting was superb—too easy, the way my granddad told it. One of them would drive the wagon through the little pockets of open country back of the Palisades while the other walked ahead, with the dog and the gun, popping whatever got up. "We'd cross the river on a Friday night and come back Monday morning with the spring wagon groaning. We got two bits apiece for the bigger birds, and a nickel each for the little fellas."

To me, at the age of ten, it sounded like heaven on earth.

"Do you still have that shotgun?" I asked hopefully.

"No," my granddad said, rolling another cigarette. He was a lean, leathery old man already in his seventies, with hard gray eyes, a thin scar of a mouth, nicotine-stained fingers, and a great, gritty fund of stories. He would live to be eighty-seven, and rise up from his death bed on the final morning of his life to shave himself with his cut-throat straight razor, having reshingled his roof, unaided, only a few weeks before. "And even if I did still have that old iron," he added, "I'd dassent give it to you. Your ma would never forgive me."

· · · · ·

Clearly I would have to seek elsewhere for a shotgun, and when I'd found it, keep any knowledge of the gun or of my hunting adventures from my tender-hearted, gun-hating mother. The few birds and rabbits I'd killed so far with the bow, I'd cooked and eaten out in the fields where I shot them. My friends and I filched lard, salt, and matches from home, a little bit at a time, and kept them hidden in a "fort" we had dug on the prairie. We dug it into a side hill, roofed it over with scrap lumber we swiped from a nearby building project (already the prairie was being nibbled to death by post-war housing development), and laid thick slabs of bluestem sod over the boards. We salvaged a rusty old frying pan from the town dump, cleaned it up with bootlegged Brillo pads, added an old-fashioned stoneware coffee pot one of the gang found in his attic, hauled water-smoothed rocks up from the river to build a fireplace, and were snug as jolly plainsmen in our splendid hideaway. It had everything a boy could desire—including a huge stack of mouldy comic books. Everything but a gun and a couple of bird dogs.

Enter Rusty and Belle.

They came trotting up to the hidden entrance of our our fort one hot September Saturday when a couple of us were boiling some crayfish we'd caught in the river. Crayfish were called "crabs" in those parts, and they were a pretty big subspecies, some of them six or eight inches long. We caught them with a hunk of liver tied to a piece of butcher's string and dangled near their holes in the shallows, under the river rocks. You let them glom on, hoisted them gently up near the top of the water, then netted them with your baseball cap. We boiled them up in an old Maxwell House coffee can, after letting them soak for about an hour or so in clear, cold water to clean the mud out of their systems. When they were done, they turned red as lobsters. We cracked them open with stones, sprinkled salt on the pieces, and scoffed them down, sometimes with crackers and peanut butter for dessert.

Snuffle, snuffle, snuffle. We saw two big, square, wet noses poking into the doorway. Nostrils big as gun muzzles, flexing open and shut as they sniffed the delicious smells.

"Cripes, it's a couple of dogs."

"I know them," Danny said. "They're Rusty and Belle. I think they're called Irish setters."

My ears perked up. A setter was a hunting dog. I'd never seen the Irish variety, though.

"Hand me my bow and quiver," I said.

"You're not gonna shoot 'em, are you?"

"No, asshole. I'm gonna see if they know how to hunt."

I brought out some crabmeat and a handful of Saltines for the dogs. They accepted the snacks eagerly and looked up for more.

"You've got to earn it," I told them. I strung the bow—I'd graduated to a thirty-five pound Osage-orange longbow by this time—nocked a homemade flu-flu arrow, and headed off at a trot toward where I'd seen a small family group of prairie chickens only about an hour ago. We were hunting into the wind, so the bird scent would blow back down to the dogs. The only trouble was that they stayed right at my heels. No good, I thought. I want them out in front. I stopped. Rusty stopped too, and looked up at me. His eyes held the big question. *What do you want, Boss?*

"Go ahead," I said, gesturing with my free hand. "Hunt 'em up!"

Belle responded first to my command, suddenly lighting up and hunting forward on a zigzag line with her head high, sucking in the hot autumn wind. Rusty took off after her, quartering in counterpoint to her course. Whenever they got more than fifteen yards ahead of me, I whistled them back, then sent them out again. I don't believe they had ever been trained to this, but they must have had at least a smidgen of hunting instinct left, though I've read since that the breed had gone almost exclusively to bench stock by then. The red gods were certainly feeling benevolent that day, to send me by sheerest chance these eager, alert, glossy-red bird dogs.

Suddenly Belle stopped. Her broad-feathered tail went up. Her head poised flat and rock-steady, almost snakelike, angling slightly downward and ahead of her. By God she was on point!

Foolishly, I ran in ahead of her in my eagerness, and the whole flock of chickens erupted at once, a great rattling blur of brown and white. I snapped an arrow after them but missed miserably. The birds flew on, fast and low, a few strong wingbeats, then a long gliding pause, then a few more wingbeats, until they were just dots at the far end of the prairie.

I couldn't bring myself to look at Belle, who I was sure must be furious at me for blowing the shot. But she wasn't. She looked delighted with herself, smirking and pirouetting like a wanton minx. She and Rusty hunted on. We pushed through the tall golden grass toward where the birds had pitched in.

About halfway there, Belle pointed again. This time I kept my head, walking in slowly ahead of her with the arrow nocked firmly and the bow held crosswise at waist height. A large, long-tailed bird suddenly scuttled ahead a few steps and took wing. A pheasant! A big, slow, greenheaded, white-necked, bronze gleaming cockbird, cackling metallically as he lifted off. I drew, fired and hit him, and he tumbled end for end into the grass as feathers drifted off downwind. Rusty, who had been to one side, was on him like a crimson flash. I ran up quickly, not knowing if Rusty would run off with the bird to eat it, and while he was still wrestling with it, got it away from him and wrung its neck. I praised them both to the skies and they wagged their tails in doggy delight. It was my first ringneck ever, and only a lucky hit at the base of the left wing accounted for our bagging it. On the way back to the fort, Belle jumped a rabbit which I also managed to kill. A great day! I rewarded my newfound friends with a fair share of the rabbit meat when we fried it up that afternoon in our underground hideaway.

Later that fall, I arranged to buy a beat-up old single-barreled, 28-gauge Savage Model 220 from a kid in my grade at school. The gun was choked Improved Cylinder and had a 28-inch barrel. Ron's dad was a wealthy doctor who spoiled him rotten, and had just bought him a 16-gauge "Eagle Grade" L.C. Smith. I gave Ron eight dollars for the Savage—money I'd been paid by neighbors for mowing lawns and shoveling snow, hard-earned every penny of it. Ron threw in three boxes of low-base $7\frac{1}{2}$s and one of high-brass 6s, along with a can of Hoppe's nitro solvent and a cleaning rod. No contemporary gun deal in the streets of Miami or Harlem ever went down more surreptitiously.

I couldn't bring the gun home for fear my parents would discover it—my mom was an inveterate snoop, always poking around in my room while I was at school to see what I'd been up to. So I wrapped the Savage in oily rags and kept it, during the week, in the fort. That didn't work for long. Every minute of every day, I was afraid some tramp would wander up from the Milwaukee Road right-of-way just across the river and find the fort. He'd swipe my gun and hold up a bank, or something. It was driving me nuts. My schoolwork also suffered.

I had a friend named Harry who lived near the grade school, and I prevailed on him to let me hide the shotgun in his garage. There were fields across the road from the school, just like the ones across from my house, and I figured to do some hunting there after school or on the weekends. Rusty and Belle had taken to following me to school that fall, hanging out in the playground during class hours and playing "keep away" with us during recess or the noon hour. Once they saw, smelled, and heard the gun go off, they were even more strongly bonded to me. I've often wondered what their rightful owners thought they were up to during those long, long absences from home.

It took a lot of trial and error—more of the latter than the former—to perfect a decent shooting style with the Savage. But my experience in wingshooting with the bow stood me in good stead. The bow had taught me how to swing with a rising bird, and keep swinging as I released the shot. With the shotgun, I had a tendency to overlead birds—especially rising woodcock, which have a disconcerting habit of pausing at the top of the rise before zigzagging out on the level through the tops of a cover. Pheasants were easy—slow, loud, straightaway fliers. Ruffed grouse were harder, startling to the point of paralysis in the racket they made getting up, then lining out low or with a tree between them and the gun, denying me a shot either way.

I wouldn't shoot at a really low bird for fear of hitting one of the dogs. I also swore off rabbits for the same reason. I could never break Rusty and Belle of tear-assing off after every bunny they jumped, like greyhounds at a dogtrack. Once Belle ran a bunny into a long piece of drainage pipe, wide enough for the rabbit but not for the dog. Rusty figured out instantly what was happening and leaped to the far end of the pipe, just in time to intercept the panicky rabbit when it emerged a moment later, still at full gallop. The gluttonous mutts quickly ripped it apart and ate it. I figured this must be the way they hunted before they took up with me. Old habits die hard.

No, they weren't perfect gun dogs by any means. In addition to eating perhaps one in every five birds I killed, they had a tendency to take off suddenly for parts unknown in the middle of a hunt, sometimes not returning until the next day. Rusty was a car chaser, and Belle a cat chaser. They inevitably took on any skunk they happened across, with predictably malodorous results. Fortunately we lived too far south for porcupines. Once they tackled a big boar raccoon, and before they learned their lesson both of them had deep gashes in their noses, flanks, and bellies that put them out of action for the better part of a week.

But now and then they were splendid. I'll never forget a double point that occurred one November afternoon in the fields across the railroad tracks. We'd been puddle jumping mallards along the river, with only sporadic success, when Belle—who had the better nose—suddenly lit up. I followed her into the wind, away from the river, across the tracks, and into a low, damp swale that gave way to cattails before rising again to a farmer's planting of field corn. At the edge of the swale she froze on point. Rusty pussyfooted up behind her, then looked to his left. Sniffed a couple times. He angled over in that direction about ten yards and locked up.

Could be the same bird, I thought. A runner, moving ahead of Belle's point. But when I went in ahead of Belle, a woodcock got up right under her nose. As I mounted the gun, I heard and then saw from the corner of my eye a big cock pheasant vault skyward from Rusty's point—no doubt flushed by the piping of the woodcock's wing feathers. It was one of those bright, cold, cobalt-blue Wisconsin afternoons—no wind, sunlight gleaming on the dogs' rich mahogany-colored fur, the field corn pale yellow in the background, the cock pheasant resplendent in full flight.

"I'll kill 'em both!" I thought as the flight paths of woodcock and ringneck momentarily crossed. I shot in that instant. Both birds fell.

That's gunning at its best.

. . . . .

Rusty and Belle disappeared from my life that winter, with the arrival of the first deep snows that put an end to the bird shooting. I have no idea what became of them. Maybe their owner moved away. Maybe they died—both of them were reckless enough. Whatever it was, I'm sure it had nothing to do with a loss of interest in hunting. I've never met a keener pair of gun dogs—nonstop, indefatigable. I'll always be grateful to them for infecting me with that enthusiasm when it counted the most.

My mother never learned of Rusty and Belle—not until I told her about them, years later, toward the end of her life.

"Where did you develop this unhealthy passion for blood sports?" she asked me one afternoon when I was visiting from my home in the East. "You never got it from me or your father."

I told her the story, just about the way I've told it here. Her eyes began to fill with tears, and suddenly I was sorry I'd confessed. I looked out the front window, across the street. It was wall-to-wall suburbia now, clear down to the river. Not an acre of native prairie left.

"If I'd known it meant so much to you, I would have allowed you to hunt," she said. "Better that than keep it hidden from me all those years."

Fat chance, I thought. Don't feel sorry for her, feel sorry for what's gone. She just doesn't get it. None of them do. They never will.

Dan O'Brien lives in the Black Hills of South Dakota with his wife, Kris, where they hunt birds with shotguns and falcons over pointing dogs. He has received awards for his writing, including the Iowa Short Fiction Award, Western Writer's Best First Novel Award, an honorary Ph.D. in literature, and two NEA Fellowships for fiction. His books are, Spirit of the Hills *and* Center of the Nation, *both novels,* The Rites of Autumn, *a falconer's journey across the American west, non-fiction, and* Eminent Domain, *short stories.*

JAKE

by Dan O'Brien

Since my wife and I have been together there have been several dogs in our household and Kris has loved them all. When we first met, her attraction for dogs was indiscriminate, embracing schizophrenic Pomeranians as passionately as finely focused English pointers. This, I felt sure, had to do with the fact that she had never seen a dog doing what a dog does best, hunting. I'd like to think it was my influence that created in Kris an understanding and love for hunting dogs, what they do, and how they can enrich your life. But, in fact, I was only a minor player in Kris's discovery. The real credit goes to Jake, who knew her long before I was on the scene.

You see, Kris was raised in southern California. She'd never been hunting, never fired a gun, never seen a well-trained dog locate, point, or retrieve a bird. But despite this disadvantage she was naturally drawn to dogs. One of the first things that attracted me to her was the eighty-pound black Lab golden retriever cross that had been her companion through four years of medical school. One of the first serious things she ever said to me was that she wouldn't have made it through school if it hadn't been for Jake.

He was with her the whole way, bounced around from city to city, keeping her company when she was studying, and sometimes waiting inside sixteen hours at a stretch until she could get home to walk him. She went to school at Dartmouth and told me that some nights, when she got home, the combination of long hours and subzero temperatures conspired to depress her to the point of tears. But Jake was always there to greet her and they walked every night and that's what gave her the strength to get up the next morning and do it again. The fact that she had learned the restorative powers of a relationship with a dog made me know she was special. And the fact that Jake had been the one to teach her, made him special too. They got me thinking that my dream of finding a woman who would enjoy life afield with me and a dog might not be completely farfetched.

· · · · ·

Jake got his looks from his Lab side. Except for slightly longer hair you'd have never known he wasn't pure Lab. He was one of those blocky dogs with a head like chiseled granite and had that gentle way of looking at you—like he felt vaguely sorry for you, being human and all. Like so many of the really good dogs, Jake seemed to know how he could best support the people with whom he lived. After Kris moved on to her internship and residency, where she had even less time, and I started hanging around, Jake shifted a portion of his allegiance to me.

I'm sure he knew it was what Kris wanted and I was grateful to be included.

Kris was doing a two-year residency in Denver and I took to spending a lot of time there. I was used to sleeping alone and while sharing a bed with Kris was a welcome change, sharing a bed with Kris and Jake was not exactly what I had in mind. I

remember coming face to face with Jake one of those first nights, when I pulled the covers back to get into bed, and thinking that I should throw him out. But he stared at me unflinchingly and I realized that this was not my call. I was the interloper here and was infringing on the unity of a serious, well-functioning team. I never saw anyone work as hard as Kris. Except for Jake, she had been alone in a seven-year battle to make something special of her life. Jake stayed on the bed.

I tried to understand what they had both been through. I found that Kris was gone a great deal, fourteen-hour days and on all-night call every third night. Jake and I were thrown together and it was good for both of us. Her house was on a busy street. The traffic was confining—something I was not used to. For good reason, Jake had seldom been off a leash and I seized this depravation as an excuse for us to escape the city.

We began going on extended walks in more remote places than Jake was used to. Kris was a little protective of him— suggesting that he wouldn't eat dog food without cooking oil over it and that November water was too cold for him to retrieve sticks from. She made it sound a little like Jake preferred tofu to T-bones but after I started taking him to my home on a South Dakota ranch, inhabited by a new English setter puppy named Idaho Spud and an ancient basset hound named Morgan, I came to know something for sure about Jake that I had suspected all along.

Morgan had run rabbits every day since his retirement several years before. He was like an old demented pensioner returning to the office out of habit. He got up early, had a little drink of water, and usually struck a trail about seven thirty. He'd run rabbits until the heat of the day. Then he'd come into the barn for another drink and snooze until four o'clock when he'd go back at it for another couple hours. A little after dark he'd come in to eat and sleep, and it would start all over again about seven the next morning. He was slow and inefficient. But he took his work seriously and didn't pay much attention to this big, black city dog who stayed in the house. But I noticed that Jake watched Morgan from the kitchen window. I caught him several times studying the old timer as he snooped through the grown-over farm equipment, and it wasn't long before the big head stiffened and the black ears came up at the sound of Morgan's strike.

Jake was aloof when it came to my hunting dogs but he couldn't help keeping an eye on Spud as we went through yard training and limited recall quail work. This whole scene, with its cacophony of new smells, made him a little nervous and he disdained close contact with these dogs. But he was interested. When Kris came out to the ranch and made a fuss over these two ruffians, it threw Jake into a tailspin. It was about that time that Kris began to take an interest herself. In me, I suppose, but more in the elements of my life. She asked about the roading harness, the electronic collar, the dog boxes in the back of the pickup. She inspected the kennel, and though I knew she had a hard time understanding the reasoning behind this way of keeping dogs, she never made any judgments. She had seen Spud pointing a wing and was fascinated by the way this little moron puppy went so deadly serious over a game. She watched steady old Morgan going about his chores and began to see how important all this was to me.

After about the third visit she wondered if, the next time we went to the ranch, she couldn't try shooting a shotgun and I, of course, bent over backwards to comply. I planned to let her shoot my side-by-side twenty but my hired hand and comrade of twenty years shook his head. "That's a mistake," he said. "She won't hit anything and that little thing will kick her silly." When Kris arrived at the ranch for her first shooting lesson we had a brand new Remington 1100 12-gauge with a shortened stock and butt pad waiting for her. She broke the first three clay pigeons she ever saw.

But, before there was any shooting, we had to put Jake in the basement. Though he had never seen a gun before, he was shy of explosions. Apparently Fourth of July fireworks had rattled him. Kris told me every year he spent most of the Fourth trying to get under the refrigerator. I had a hard time believing it. With little Spud pistoning in his kennel and poor old blind Morgan limping out to investigate every dead clay pigeon, it was hard to imagine that a dog like Jake wouldn't be clambering to get in on the fun. But he sure wasn't.

Kris and I came into the house full of good thoughts about the possibility of Kris going pheasant hunting. The season was half over by then but there might be a way to do some late season hunting. She was delighted with the shotgun and the shooting. I was delighted that she was delighted. She even mentioned the idea that Jake might go with us on the pheasant hunt. I knew that notion made sense to her but I tried to gently discourage it. I restated my theory that house dogs don't make good bird dogs and bird dogs don't make good house dogs. She looked at me oddly and said simply that I underestimated dogs. I know now she spoke from a native understanding, but then, I suppose, I only smiled.

When we went down into the basement we found Jake quaking in a corner. It was a terrible sight and Kris was upset so I didn't say anything like "I told you so." When she put her arms around him and apologized for shooting I knew the plans for a pheasant hunt were in jeopardy. I felt my dream of having a woman to share my days in the field slipping away. But it was a dream worth dreaming and—theories be damned—I made myself a promise to fight for it.

Thank God Jake loved cheese more than he feared anything.

Kris was skeptical, but after Jake figured out that the sound of the cap gun wrapped in a towel meant cheddar, it wasn't long until the towel was discarded. Another week and you didn't want to be between him and the kitchen when the starter's pistol went off. Finally he'd come full bore across any field for a 12-gauge—and a quarter pound of gouda.

So I figured we at least had a chance. Dog over his gun shyness, new shotgun, first-time hunter, this had the potential to be fun. Kris was very excited about the possibility of bagging a few pheasants. She had recipes she wanted to try and the idea of Jake becoming a focused bird dog, though I downplayed it, thrilled her.

· · · · ·

But there was another catch. On a picnic, during a rare medical school break, when Jake was just a puppy, he had wandered off and been caught in a chicken coop, knee deep in fresh plucked chickens. Kris said it was the first time he had ever seen birds up close but the owner of the chickens was not in a forgiving mood and whacked Jake across the nose. "He hasn't shown much interest in birds since," Kris said.

She swore the punishment had only been one crisp thump across the muzzle so I assured her that there was no problem. Jake didn't mind gunfire now and he loved to retrieve. His natural instincts would take over and he'd do fine. That's what I told her. But I'd gotten to know Jake pretty well by then and knew he learned lessons for keeps. I was worried that his desire to do what people wanted him to do might very well extend to that New Hampshire farmer. In an attempt to avoid a bad day in the field, when we did finally take Jake out, I dug a Hungarian partridge out of the freezer—partridge caddis can be a hot trout fly in the Black Hills—and thawed it one morning when Kris was at work. That afternoon I went into the backyard where Jake and I normally played fetch with tennis balls and sticks.

He leaped and twisted with joy when I held the stick over his head but sat, trembling with anticipation, when I gave the command. I threw the stick twice and he pounded after it, delivering it to hand when I asked. The third time I surreptitiously substituted the partridge from my pocket for the stick and sent him off after it with an encouraging "fetch." He bore down on it like a goshawk but never laid a tooth on it. As soon as he recognized it as a bird he pulled up like it was a cow pie and trotted quickly back to my side. He looked up at me like I'd pulled the dirtiest trick in the book and I knew I had a problem.

But by this time Kris was counting on a pheasant hunt so I reassured Jake by putting my arm around him. But that didn't help much. The nervous look in his eye told me that I'd better quickly get him back into retrieving or I'd have an even bigger problem on my hands. I went back to the house for his favorite toy—a green Day-glo Frisbee—and this snapped him out of his paranoia. He did the happy dog dance complete with leaps and yips and I sailed the Frisbee out for him to chase. He was a pro—a veteran of San Diego beaches and Ivy League campuses—and made a long graceful lunge, picking the Frisbee neatly out of midair. It dawned on me that this might be the key.

I found a roll of duct tape under the seat of my pickup and, out of Jake's sight, taped the partridge to the top of the Frisbee. Then, in my most affected, excited voice, I encouraged Jake in his own excitement. I held the Frisbee above him—with the partridge safely on top and out of sight—and he again leaped and yipped. And when I sent it wobbling out into the yard he charged after it as usual. But when he came close, he jumped back like he'd found a rattlesnake. Still, he knew the Frisbee was there and wanted badly to bring it back. He didn't return to my side but sat down looking at the problem. Finally he reached out and, with his lips curled delicately back, took the very edge of the Frisbee in his teeth and drug the whole works back to lay at my feet. Never did he, in any way, come in contact with a feather.

We had to start with a single tail feather taped to the Frisbee and work up through two feathers, one wing, two wings, and eventually a whole bird. But in a week he was over his dread of dead birds. It took another two weeks and a very tolerant pigeon to get him to put a moving feathered object into his mouth. But once he caught on, he was a natural. In no time, he was making seventy-five-yard blind retrieves and doing it with extreme enthusiasm.

· · · · ·

While all this was going on I was working with Spud, getting him ready for his first exposure to pheasants. I didn't expect much from such a pup but figured him to put a few birds up. I ran the two dogs together on a route that included several stock dams and, of course, Jake would dive headlong into each dam as we came to it. If it was a hot day, he'd swim around for five or ten minutes and Spud, who was still only a year old, got so he'd follow Jake right on in. To this day Spud is the swimmingest setter I've ever seen and I attribute that to Jake.

In a lot of ways Jake was Spud's hero during that first summer and fall of life, but I wondered what Spud would think of his idol if he failed to retrieve a shot bird or, worse yet, just stuck close to Kris and didn't hunt. Spud has always been a go-getting bird dog and I had no worries that he wouldn't hunt hard. His problem, if anything, would be overzealousness and that is a good kind of problem to have. Jake, on the other hand, might decide he didn't go for this rowdy life and quit. I was afraid that he might influence Kris to do the same.

In the days before our pheasant hunt I got worried that Jake and Kris would have a bad day. Experienced hunters know that bad days happen and that you should just forget them. If the dog screws up or you can't shoot well, put it behind you—things will be better next time. But a bad day could be fatal for a thirty-year-old with high expectations of hunting with her faithful old house dog—both for the first time. And I didn't want Kris's interest to die. I knew if it did, my life would veer from its ideal path and I'd find myself hunting mostly solo.

So the importance of the pheasant hunt began to take on cosmic proportions and by the time the day arrived I was a worried wreck, and Jake must have been getting tired of retrieving that same duct-taped pigeon—with one wing left loose to flap. I had done everything I could but still I was not confident. I worried about Jake drawing a tough old rooster with only a broken wing for his first retrieve, I worried about Kris's shooting, I worried that I wouldn't be able to resist kibitzing.

By the time everything was ready it was late in the season and the wild birds had been worked over pretty hard. In an effort to control some of the variables, I chose a hunting preserve owned by a friend as the venue for our outing. Twenty dollars a bird seemed awfully high but my friend guaranteed there would be birds out there, and I reasoned that the team I was bringing—Kris, Jake, Spud, and myself—was not exactly a well-oiled hunting machine that could run up a huge bill.

The day dawned gray and overcast and low, flat clouds threatened rain. It was not the kind of day I'd hoped for but the weather report was for clearing with a light, warm breeze. I offered up a little prayer to Orion as I loaded Spud into his dog box. Jake had had only a few lessons in kenneling into a dog box, but he loaded all right and we were on the road by eight o'clock.

Kris was nearing the end of her residency and we had begun to talk about what would happen the next year. There were job opportunities in California, Chicago, about any big city, but she didn't want to go there. She had come to like South

Dakota and thought she liked the kinds of things we were doing that day. I looked at the sky as we pulled into my friend's shooting reserve. There was a faint streak of blue directly overhead, but the horizons were still caulk and snow was still not out of the question.

My friend pointed us down the road to a half section of thick brome grass and old weedy milo fields along the edge of standing corn. There was a marshy spot there too, and cattails grew thick below a large stock dam from which we could hear the sounds of geese and mallards. We unloaded near the standing corn but, when we started out, I pointed Spud in the other direction. I knew there would be birds in the corn and if he got in there all we'd see would be roosters spiraling up like distant missiles.

I carried a gun but wasn't out to shoot. I hoped Spud would find a few birds and maybe flash point one or two. What I was really there for was to see to it that Kris had a good time. But it started out poorly. A rooster jumped at her feet before we were thirty yards from the truck and she fired twice before the stock had even touched her shoulder. She probably fired fifteen feet over the bird. Jake didn't flinch at the shots but didn't pay much attention to the bird either. Spud chased it out of sight.

While we waited for the little imp to return—which he did in fifteen minutes with his tongue nearly dragging—I tried to keep Kris's mood light. She's a competitive person and was used to breaking clay pigeons. She was instantly mad at herself for missing—the beginner's mistake—and I was afraid it would affect her whole day. I seldom care if a bird comes to bag, but that day it seemed crucial. I laughed it off, "Everybody misses, forget it. Take your time. You got lots of time." And the more I talked the more I knew it was the wrong thing to do. I had to force myself to shut up. We waited in silence and Jake laid down at Kris's feet. When Spud finally returned, Jake got up and sniffed the huffing Spud as if to ask what the big deal was.

We set off again, walking along the edge of the cattails and the sky began to clear. The winter browns went rich with shadow and we both praised the changing weather. Suddenly it was pleasant just walking there with Kris. This was more like my dream. Spud was somewhere in the next county but I wasn't going to let that spoil the day. Jake had begun to potter ahead of us and it was possible he might stumble onto a pheasant. Kris and I were both beginning to stop trying so hard and enjoy the day when Spud angled in from somewhere and flushed a pheasant twenty-five yards to our left.

I didn't even pull up on it. It was out a good ways and one of those tough crossing shots. But Kris brought her gun up and poked a shot at it. I winced when I saw the gun barrel stop just before she shot. The bird was going forty miles an hour by then. She missed it by a mile. "You got to keep the gun moving," I said before I thought to say it diplomatically.

Kris frowned. "I don't know about this," she said. It was in the tone of voice I had dreaded for weeks and I felt a touch of panic. It was me. I was making her crazy.

"Look," I said. "Spud is running amok. I'm going to take him up in that brome grass where I can keep an eye on him. You take Jake and walk up to the dam, then back through the cattails. There should be birds in the cattails for sure."

I gathered Spud up and headed out. I figured the only chance was to leave her alone and hope the improving weather would work its magic. As I started uphill toward the brome bench I saw Jake watching me. He looked from me to Kris and back again. At the time I thought he was just confused about our splitting up. But now, I think he had sensed the tension in the air. I believe he was evaluating things—trying to understand what was at stake.

· · · · ·

The day won me over. As soon as I started to concentrate on Spud, everything mellowed. He was wearing down and I stayed on him until he was quartering in front of me fairly well. We worked up through the brome for a quarter mile and he bumped a pheasant. I whoaed him and got in to where I could praise him. After we made the turn and started back he hit another one and held it until I was in range. When it came up, I shot and killed Spud's first bird.

We celebrated with a good petting in the dry grass and for an instant I forgot about Kris and Jake. But when we got walking again, there was still a nagging feeling in the back of my head and when we came to where we could look down on the cattail slough I was holding my breath, hoping Kris and Jake were not back at the pickup.

They were still hunting the cattails and I resisted going down to join them. Spud and I sat down in the golden grass above them and watched. They didn't really know where to look for birds and they wandered to areas that seldom hold them. It was all I could do not to shout directions from my hill. But Jake was out front and quartering within range and they looked happy enough. I had Spud on a lead and we settled in to enjoy watching the woman I loved work her first cattail slough with her pet retriever. I was afraid it would look like Abbott and Costello on a hunt. But they didn't look too bad. Their demeanor had changed since I'd last seen them. They were concentrating on what they were doing yet casual and relaxed. Something magic had happened in my absence and I saw an ease in Kris's walk that I'd never seen before, but have seen a thousand times since.

They were certainly pushing birds in front of them and, the way they were working the slough, they might just run into a herd of them at the end where they'd have to fly or run across a dirt road. There was a particular corner of firebush that looked great and Jake was leading Kris right to it.

I sat up a little as they approached the firebush. It looked like Jake's gait picked up. His tail was ringing! He began to bounce and up came a bird. Bang—and it folded. I couldn't believe it. It was beautiful. Jake charged into the brush and brought the bird to Kris. I could hear her squeal with delight.

But Jake just spit it into her hand and dove back into the bush. Up came another pheasant. Bang. Another perfect retrieve. Back into the bushes. Two birds. Bang, bang! and Kris stopped to reload while Jake searched out the birds.

Then birds were coming up everywhere. Bang! Bang! Kris had two more down before the rocketing pheasants turned into twenty-dollar bills in my mind. I struggled to my feet. "Wait." But Jake was still working the brush and I hustled toward them with Spud straining at the leash.

When I got there, Kris had six birds lined up at her feet. The gun was empty and she was kneeling with her arms around a panting, very happy retriever. She beamed up at me and I beamed back.

For weeks afterward all she could talk about was how great the hunt had been. Winter set in with a vengeance then and we didn't get a chance to go hunting again that year. But she was hooked deep. We lived off that day for months and it became part of our history, part of what makes us what we are.

Old Morgan died not long after and, though you always take the death of a good dog hard, we knew it was his time and he'd lived a full life. The real shock came early that spring, just after Kris and I decided to make our desire to spend the rest of our lives together official. It was the spring of Kris's last year of residency and we planned to get married and live in South Dakota where the whole bunch of us could enjoy a little more freedom than most people are used to.

Jake had not seemed his old self for a couple days and we took him to the vet's for a checkup. The vet wanted to keep him overnight for some tests and we really didn't think too much of it. But early in the morning—it was a Sunday because Kris was home—he called to say that Jake had died. Kris was speechless and handed the phone to me.

I listened dumbfounded while this perfectly nice young vet tried to explain. He was terribly upset and obviously had no idea what had really happened. I listened to him rattle on, searching for the explanation he never found. The cause of death was unknown. But I knew why Jake was dead. It all fell into place for me that morning and the knowledge changed my life.

Jake died because his job was done. He'd seen Kris through medical school, her internship, and her residency— been there through some rough and lonely times. He'd brought her from a college girl to a woman aware of so much more. He led her through important stages of her life and he led her through that cattail slough and into that flock of pheasants. He'd eased her gently into a new, more vital life and he was counting on me to take it from there.

It was a terribly sad time in our lives and most of the day I held Kris, and rocked her, and tried my best to make her see what Jake had given her. But his gifts were not only for Kris. I've come to know that he gave a great deal to me too. He made a dream come true.

Now Kris and I gun for pheasant, and grouse and woodcock and quail and partridge. We do it with joy and reverence. And we do it with good birds dogs that live like Jake always did. Idaho Spud is older now and has been joined by Old Hemlock Melville who is learning the trade and promises to carry on a tradition. They both live in the house. They sleep on our bed with us, and some nights, when Spud is hard beside me and Mel is pressing against Kris and they are both rolling the blanket under them and shrink-wrapping Kris and me closer and closer, I think this is the way Jake wanted it all along. His big square head with the deep, dark eyes floats through my dreams. His wisdom haunts me.

Glen Sheppard, a newspaperman for forty years, was raised hunting birds and chasing trout and bluegills in northern Michigan. Since 1969 he has published The North Woods Call *from the drumlins along Lake Michigan near Charlevoix. Sometimes described as the bible of Michigan conservation, the bi-weekly newspaper highlights exclusive conservation and outdoor recreation reports. Mary Lou and Shep share life with a bird dog named Nails and a retriever named Rusty. "Toots, 1975-85" is etched into a bluebird house made of mahogany on a post near the barn.*

TOOTS

by Glen Sheppard

It was a Christmas Eve in the 1950s when I realized
that bird dogs would dominate life.

I'd gone down the line talking to each guy. Their
attitudes ranged from bitter to depressed. They'd counted
on being freshly showered, in clean uniforms, warm and
well fed—maybe even enjoying the afterglow of a few
beers—and taking in the Bob Hope Christmas show.

It hadn't turned out that way.

They talked about family and sweethearts. About the big Christmas meal. The decorations and the tree. How they'd kick back in a big, warm, soft chair after Christmas dinner and sleep the rest of the day away. How, if they wanted to, they'd take a shower in the morning, another in the evening, and change their socks and underwear twice a day. Exactly the kind of visions young American men should be having on a Christmas eve in a cold, dreary foxhole.

Back at my position, I hunkered down to catch some sleep. It was going to be a long and, with any luck, boring night. When the radio guy shook me awake to tell me the squad was ready for patrol, I was sitting on a stump along a tote road in northern Michigan's Dead Stream Swamp. The leaves were down. Everything was brown, yellow, or conifer-green. I was rubbing my dog's ear. As I came out of the grog, I realized my right hand was stroking a gas mask bag in which I kept tobacco, candy bars, and a book, thinking it was a dog.

That nagged at me as the squad fell in and we headed into the night. Everyone else was trying to escape their reality by filling their minds with loving faces, a warm, cheerful home, mounds of hot food, and clean bodies and clothes.

Not me. I'm sitting on a stump talking to a dog.

Clearing my head for the business at hand, I vowed to never again be without a dog and to do as much October stump sitting as possible.

And I have.

Early on I became bullheaded about that sorta stuff. Bird dogs are English setters. It may be the best hunter in the township, but if it ain't an English setter it is just another dog, no matter how good it hunts or behaves. Nothing against it, but it isn't a bird dog. You hunt birds with guns that have two barrels. No matter how deadly you are with it, if it has only one tube it isn't fit for hunting birds. (You fish trout only with long rods made of cane.) Birds are ruffed grouse and woodcock. Pheasants, quail, and other game that fly are whatever they are named, but they aren't "birds."

Dad used to brag that "I'm too smart to be dumb enough to think I'll ever understand women." Time taught me he might better have been talking about bird dogs. (But, maybe, he

The English Setter—A Breed Apart
by Bruce Langton
Published in a limited edition of 950 by Countrysport, Inc.

The Labrador Retreiver—A Breed Apart
by Bruce Langton
Published in a limited edition of 950 by Countrysport, Inc.

wasn't that smart.) It took many frustrating, teeth-gnashing, larynx-strained years to figure out that if you take a dog too seriously, demand that she do it your way ("right"), she's gonna make a fool of you. And, more important, you aren't going to like her or yourself.

Look for a pup that comes from pure hunting stock. From parents that live for the hunt. Don't give a hoot about their pedigree or how stylish or colorful they are. Just that their

brains are in their nose and their hearts are stuffed with grouse and woodcock feathers. Their instincts will handle the rest.

Get 'em young. As young as possible, but never over eight weeks old. Teach them the rudiments. But make it fun. Always remember that bird hunting is supposed to be a happy game. That's what the pup must learn from day one. There are no scores in this business. No losers. If you spend time together where birds live you're winners. (Remember: God was at his best when he made the places where brook trout and ruffed grouse live.)

The hard part comes next and you need a special housemate to make it work. The first day the pup is with you, make it a partner. I mean, be serious about it: take the little critter to bed with you for the first couple of weeks. (Synchronize your turnovers so you don't squash the pup.) Not only does this bond you, it potty trains the pup in a hurry. The pup won't do it in bed, so it will let you know when the time has come, allowing the two of you to scoot outside.

We, finally, got this down pat in July of 1975. That's when Toots came to us. I'd lost Thorne the previous winter and had been looking for a replacement. I found her in a big litter in the Upper Peninsula of Michigan. I forget how many pups there were, but at four weeks they were already on the bottle. The mother couldn't keep up.

Previously, I'd agonized over several litter picks. Not Toots. As many choices as there were, somehow the eyes, the spinning wormy little tail, the confidence displayed in her eager curiosity, and the flat head with a long, squarish nose and jaw sent an instant signal. At that age she was pure white. I prefer white dogs, easier to see when working. Her parents were mostly white, with flecks of blue, gray, and amber. (She would end up with a few splotches of tan.)

Jack Jorgenson, a state waterways supervisor, wanted her gone, now. He was over his head hand feeding them. It was risky, but she was no longer dependent on her mother for nourishment. Jorgenson directed us to a local market for a particular type of baby formula and instructions on how to feed her. She fit easily in the pocket of my sweatshirt (reminding me of a pup from my bachelor days who lived part time in the half-open bottom drawer of a newsroom desk in Detroit).

We were camping, so Toots went into the world immediately experiencing the outdoors. That first day, she alternated between snuggling, sleeping in my pocket, whining, seemingly trying to find her mother and littermates, and vomiting the formula we had to half force down her. By evening, I was on the verge of taking her back, afraid she wasn't going to make it. Mary Lou's mothering instinct and experience told her she would be just fine, once her (and my) nerves settled down and she felt secure.

That night she joined us in the big sleeping bag and soon cuddled and slept. Sometime in the night I was awakened by a sandpapery tongue on my neck. Taking her out she did her job and returned to my hands as naturally as if she'd always belonged there. Mary Lou halted my move to warm some milk for the pup.

It wasn't full daybreak when she was tugging on my ear, then nursing on a finger, not sure if she wanted to play, potty, or eat. We did all three and she never again thought she'd known another home.

By seven weeks she had mastered her manners and responded to her name, came when called, sometimes, and had destroyed a handmade pair of Indian caribou boots I'd picked up years before in Alaska. She completely ignored the cap gun I fired when she ate and played. She was alternately attacking and pointing the woodcock wing that fluttered off the end of the long fishing rod. We were still working on stop and stay. By ten weeks she lived for the woodcock wing and had made wobbly points on several birds and dozens of songbirds and butterflies. She also had stop and stay down, but it had taken some stern drill.

· · · · ·

During the bird season opener September 15, 1975, when Toots was three months old (that's right, three months), she became a legend, the standard by which I will always measure bird dogs.

About a quarter mile from our old farmhouse in the headwaters of the Elk River watershed was a feral orchard. It was flanked by a rather steep slope covered with pole-size pines. Near the center of the orchard was a tilting tool shed. The first tree south of the shed was the most productive early season apple tree in the orchard. A fine, thick old apple tree. We'd wild flushed a grouse from under the tree several times.

It was about 4:30 p.m. and I wasn't about to alert that bird again, if he was there. My plan was to sneak from the north end of the orchard, with Toots on a short leash, releasing her while we were still behind that tool shed.

I was hoping for her first kill.

Letting her loose, she dashed around the shed before I could move. Stepping briskly, I expected to hear a bird flush. Coming around the shed, there was Toots, still a scrawny pup, dead on point. The bird was not more than eight feet in front of her, on the ground, tail fanned.

The bird, a big mature male, died not fifteen feet from her nose and fell in clear view. Cracking the gun to slide another round in the empty barrel, I told her to fetch. Damn pup! She just held that silly puppy point, ignoring several demands that she fetch. As the shell dropped into the barrel I raised a boot to give her a push, not a kick.

Two birds flushed from within the tree! She hadn't broken point because she knew they were there. I got off a fast, awkward shot and dumped one of the birds at the edge of the pines. It was thrashing on the ground, out of sight.

Again, I told Toots to fetch. She was off like a streak, down the hill, then up, heading toward me, with a glob of flailing wings in a tiny mouth, her head obscured by the bird. She dropped it several times, but pounced and managed to get her mouth around it again.

I'd died and gone to bird hunter's heaven. Of course, it wasn't always, or usually, that good. How could it be?

She quickly developed several quirks. Toots was a quick character study. If she didn't like someone, she would not hunt with them. Several times, she simply trotted behind me, refusing to hunt.

She didn't like being left alone, except at home or in the car, and she'd get even if you left her in a strange place, like the motel room where she destroyed a one hundred dollar set of drapes and a bedspread, or the cabin where she mangled a screen door.

So we didn't leave her alone, which produced one of my proudest moments. Mary Lou and I were staying at the Holiday Inn in Grayling. I bumped into some friends who wanted me to join them for a presupper drink. I wasn't interested, so used the excuse that Toots was back in the room. They made some derogatory remarks about not being able to trust that lousy mutt. I told them I'd meet them in the bar. Going back to the room, I put Toots on heel. She casually followed me through the halls, ignoring every distraction. At the table in the bar I put her on sit. She sat there nearly an hour, moving only her head, eyes, and tail, with several dozen people moving and talking.

I kept hearing about that performance from other people for years.

But she wasn't perfect. She liked to point rabbits. You knew when she was on a rabbit; she would hop, stiff-legged, up and down, maybe four to six inches in the air. When the rabbit broke cover she'd ignore it.

And she never liked retrieving dead birds. If they were alive she'd grab them and bring them to you. But not dead, which led to an embarrassing moment along the Jordan River.

I still hadn't accepted this flaw. It was early season and we'd broken a young covey, downing three in, maybe, a minute or so, in a snarl of berry bushes. The second bird was thrashing. She grabbed it and I picked up the first one. Then I told her to fetch the third one, which I "knew" had fallen about twenty-five yards to the south. No way. She went and squatted beside a big boulder to the west, ignoring my repeated demands that she find the bird.

Just as I was about to lose my temper, I noticed another hunter walking toward me. Fine shooting and dog work, the elderly hunter applauded. Why are you mad at the dog? he wondered. I told him she wouldn't fetch the third bird, as we walked toward her. The bird was no more than a foot from her.

The guy, probably in his early seventies, smiled and rubbed Toots's head. He knew who had the smarts in this pair.

After that when she wouldn't fetch, I just followed her to the bird and picked it up myself. It was a small compromise to make in return for her bird-finding and bird-holding qualities.

A week hunting in the Copper Country comes to mind. We were staying in a resort about a block from downtown Copper Harbor. We would walk to the restaurant, Toots following and then sitting on the porch until we finished. Folks, including hunters, asked what kind of dog she was; they weren't familiar with bird dogs. (Retired Michigan wildlife chief Nels Johnson has a great line about the tendency of Upper Peninsula hunters to drive two-tracks and ground swat birds they see ahead of the car. "Know how they shoot trap in the UP?" Nels asks. The answer: "They put twenty-five blue rock in a grocery bag, back off twenty-five yards and open fire.")

I'd arranged to be dropped off and my car left about a mile down Brockway Mountain Road. This is rugged hunting. You must scramble over steep rock ridges. The dog can be twenty yards away, but you have to move one hundred yards to get to her.

Within the first fifteen minutes, we had killed our limit of grouse—five. Before we reached the car, we had seventeen more points. Fantastic hunting; twenty-two points in less than two hours. She held every one of those birds steady while I climbed up, down, and around those rock cliffs to get to her. (That was also the last time I allowed myself to take a limit, except on migratory woodcock.)

She was in her second year when Mary Lou wanted to see her hunt. It was the first week of October. I had parked the car at the high banks on the South Branch of the Au Sable, intending to fish for a while and then hunt. Woodcock flights were in.

Toots slid down the slope and onto the boggy bank along the river, coming to point while we were still edging down the hill. She was in the open. Easy shot. Mary Lou was right behind me, as I told her Toots had a woodcock pinned and that I would walk up until I was no more than a few feet behind her. The bird would then flush and, if it didn't fly over the river, I'd shoot it, I explained, like it was gospel.

Sure as hell. The bird flushed, leveled off at no more than fifteen feet and flew in the open along the riverbank. I emptied both barrels. The bird kept flying and then landed in brush maybe twenty yards down the river. The three of us moved up. Toots went back on point. The bird flushed. I emptied both barrels, again. The bird flew on and landed once more.

We moved up. Toots pointed. The bird flushed. I fired. Nothing. Then again, my sixth shot, at the bird flying in the open. This time it dropped, loudly flogging the ground with a busted wing. Toots fetched.

"Geez! Is it always like this? Good thing you have Toots," she quipped, between smirks.

· · · · ·

Several years later, Toots put on another all-star performance for Dad and my two youngest brothers. I'd agreed to meet them at the forks in the Dead Stream Swamp at noon. A business emergency came up and I got there about 4:00 p.m. I was surprised to see them standing around a fire, their guns stashed. It was cold and wet. They were tired and fixing to singe some steaks, which they'd brought in case there were no birds. They hadn't had a shot all day. I was surprised because flight birds were in where I live, about seventy-five miles north.

When I said I was going to hunt for a few minutes, Dad made some biting comments about wasting my time "with that dog!" Some bad experiences with wild, wide-ranging English setters had soured him.

A half hour later, I was back with four birds. We wrapped them in tinfoil with butter and onions and put them in the coals. Dad didn't comment, except that they sure made super hors d'oeuvres.

Michigan's November 15-30 deer season was hard on Toots. She couldn't understand my leaving the house with a gun and not taking her. Mary Lou said she would lay by the gun cabinet and moan until I came back. So, while I object to Michigan's December bird season, as soon as deer hunting ended I'd take her hunting daily, whenever possible, for a week or so. The shotgun was empty. But I figured I owed her that much.

One year, I had pegged the habits of a really fine buck during bird season. Thought I had him down pat. Opening day of rifle season he took on a new character. Never saw his tracks that season, but heard that someone had missed a huge thirteen pointer in the swamp south of my eighty acres.

December 1, with deer hunters out of the woods and the weather balmy for that time of year, Toots and I headed out for our charade hunt. We were in the pines below the same orchard where as a three-month-old pup she had made her fabulous emergence as a bird dog. Suddenly she started a contorted dance around a large fallen pine. She would charge toward the tree, stop, yap shrilly several times, spin around, fall back, and then charge again. After a half dozen or so charges a trophy buck calmly stood up and slowly, almost disdainfully, limped off. He'd been knocked in the right rear leg but was putting some weight on it. I could have killed him with birdshot he was so close. He had probably been hiding there for days.

She loved to go fishing with me, which came close to being our undoing. She would sit at the edge of the stream watching me cast. Fishing the Jordan in June, I spotted a steelhead in shallow water near the east shore. Clipping off the dry fly, I knotted a streamer on the 5X tippet and cast. The fish took after several casts. As it barreled out of the water, Toots nearly fell over on herself. Then, perhaps her dignity at stake, she raced into the water, yapping and following the fish as it dove and then headed upstream. I couldn't hold the fish—a six- to eight-pounder—on the light leader and four-weight rod. It broke off around a bend, with Toots in hot pursuit.

A few seconds later she came around the bend on the opposite side of the river, swimming frantically, only part of her head out of the water. The current surges through this spot in a torrent, smashing under a twenty-five- to thirty-foot-long string of cedar sweepers. It is so powerful and deep that I've never been able to rescue flies that have hung up in the sweepers. At the end of the sweepers the river rages over and down a narrow chute filled with boulders and debris that could crush man or dog.

Toots wasn't going to make it. The current was sucking her into the sweepers. Flinging the Bob Summers fly rod some men might die for onto the bank, I plunged across the stream. She disappeared under the first sweeper. An instant later I saw she had tumbled over, her legs toward the surface, her paws smashing through the cedar boughs.

If I didn't hit my head on something, I could hold my breath until I got through the sweepers. I dove, desperately lunging for her. By some miracle I, finally, got her collar. Kicking wildly, my right foot found something solid (a rock or sunken log) and I managed to propel us into the open and to the surface.

After some thrashing, my feet found the bottom and I dragged her toward shore. Finally getting my arms around her, she was limp, perhaps briefly in shock. As the water level receded to about my waist, she came alive, scrambling up my stomach until her chest was in my face, her legs around my neck.

On shore, I set her down. She stood there, legs splayed, neck and head drooping. My waders and vest pockets bulged with water. Shedding them, I sat on the bank, rubbing water out of her feathers and darn near crying as she stood there dazed. In a few seconds, she crawled into my lap and started shaking. Leaving the waders, vest, and rod, I carried her to the car. Putting her on the sweatshirt and under the old down coat I keep in the Suburban year around, I started the rear heater, even though it was June, and went back for the fishing tackle. Standing there, looking at the current slamming along the opposite bank, I realized, for the first time, neither one of us should have made it with me encumbered with the waders and packed vest.

She didn't eat for a day and a half, and rarely moved. By the third day she seemed to have recovered. Which was better than I'd done. Though I hadn't felt them during the dive into the river, I was a mass of bruises, apparently from smashing into the sweepers.

During her last season we could hunt only about an hour at a time. She was feeble, but begged to be in the field. On her last hunt we were working along a creek about a half mile south of the house, in a three-mile stretch of wild country. She'd pointed seven birds—three grouse and four woodcock. I had a grouse and two woodcock in the bag. I was ready to cross the creek and take her home before she was so weak that I had to carry her. She went on point not ten feet from the edge of the creek. She had worked the area for a couple of minutes, so I doubted a bird had suddenly materialized, but as I came up behind her a grouse flushed. I shot it. Picking it up, I waded across the creek, expecting her to follow. When she didn't I turned to call her. She was on point again. Walking back through the creek, a woodcock flushed not two feet from her nose. I shot it. I have never been able to explain to myself how those two birds suddenly materialized where she had found none seconds before and after I had milled around the area looking for a creek crossing.

From then on she was too weak. I kept the shotgun and vest in the heated portion of the garage for the rest of the season, so she wouldn't see me take them from the gun cabinet.

Irv Drost, an old hunting buddy, used to declare: "God only gives you one good woman and one good dog." Irv has a lot more experience with women than I do, so I can't comment on that (besides, what would you do with more than one?). But I've never had a bad dog and I've had many good ones.

Toots wasn't one of them.

She was majestic.

If there is a billet in heaven for old newspapermen, I expect to find her waiting for me by that stump along the long ago overgrown tote road in the Dead Stream Swamp.

Philip Bourjaily was born in Iowa City and has lived in the area all his life, with time out for high school in Barcelona, Spain, and college in Charlot, Virginia. After vigorously resisting his father's early attempts to turn him into a hunter, he took up the sport on his own after college and began writing about it shortly thereafter.

His work has appeared in Field and Stream, Sports Afield, The American Hunter, *and other national and regional publications. He is also co-author (with Vance Bourjaily) of the book* Fishing by Mail.

He lives in Iowa City with his wife, Pamela, son, Charles, and son or daughter as yet unnamed and unborn at presstime, and Sam.

SAM

by Philip Bourjaily

Somewhere up ahead I heard the very conspicuous sound of a bell not ringing. Bending over double, I ran down a deer trail through a thicket of young willows, holding the gun in one hand and fending off branches with the other—you don't want to dawdle when your dog is pointing a pheasant. Breaking into the open I found Sam standing rigid in the knee-deep grass, the tip of his tail beginning to flag. I released him with a tap on the back of the head, and he resumed the chase with me chugging along right behind him. A hundred yards down the trail he pointed again. I tapped him, he took a few mincing steps, then locked into a third point, his quivering intensity leaving no doubt the bird was right under his nose this time. The pheasant waited only a split second before flushing, but it was warning enough. I'd skidded to a halt, flicked off the safety, and was raising the gun in anticipation as the cackling rooster flew straight into the low afternoon sun. Pulling the trigger as he disappeared into the blinding glare, I was rewarded first by a heavy thump, then the sound of Sam rustling forward through the grass to make the retrieve.

You'll hear sometimes that pheasants will turn pointing dogs into nervous wrecks, running out from under the dog's noses instead of sitting obediently like proper game birds. I have to differ: Sam was born a nervous wreck, but he handles wild roosters just fine. If anything, pheasant hunting seems to calm him down.

At eight years old, Sam still has the look of a young German shorthair waiting to fill out. Until he turned five or six, people invariably guessed his age at under a year. Even today, no matter how much I feed him, I can still encircle his waist with my hands. In the past two years, however, his muzzle has turned white. What he looks like now is a year-old shorthair with a white muzzle, the white hair as much at odds with his appearance as sideburns and a mustache on a ten-year-old boy.

Nor has the passage of time conferred much in the way of wisdom or serenity upon Sam. He still barks frantically at every slow moving farm vehicle that passes by. Ditto for dinner guests. Outside, he patrols the yard at top speed and points feral cats with frightening intensity. In the house, he keeps to himself, coiled like a spring on his dog bed. Occasionally he'll check in for a quick, reassuring pat on the head, then turn around and leave the room. Only when summer thunderstorms rattle the windows does he cling near to us, trembling.

Years ago I watched Sam's grandfather, Peter Gunn, run in a shoot-to-retrieve trial with Vern Zach, the trainer who later gave Sam to me. Vern and Peter were up against another man and his setter, who were, incidentally, the only dog and owner

I've ever seen who actually did resemble one another. At the starting line, the rail-thin reddish setter whined and strained against a lead in imitation of his tall, gaunt, red-haired owner, who paced nervously while stuffing shells into a pump gun. Vern joked with the gallery, a Remington 3200 broken open over his shoulder. Peter lay at Vern's feet, regarding the other dog with drowsy contempt, on the verge, it seemed, of falling sound asleep. At the blast of the judge's whistle, Peter was transformed instantly into a ground-eating blur of energy that

outran, outhunted, and outclassed every other dog at the trial. In the field, Sam has every last ounce of Peter Gunn's drive and style. What he lacks is an "off" switch.

I have other interests besides birds and gun dogs, and while I'm sometimes a little pressed to remember what they are, I can enjoy life between pheasant hunts. Sam, on the other hand, simply marks time between outings, unaware that there will ever be an end to the cycle of running and waiting to run. I am burdened by the knowledge that these cycles are indeed finite, and I'm reminded more and more these days by that whitening muzzle that sometime soon I'll have to start thinking about the next dog.

I may not have the nerve to try my luck with another high-octane burner like Sam. He has been more of a project than any first-time trainer deserved, and our successes together were many years in coming. The rewards of hunting pheasants with a stylish, wide-ranging pointing dog are great, but so are the frustrations. I find myself torn between wanting the next dog to be an exact copy of Sam or wanting it to be his opposite in every way. I'm writing this in full knowledge of the fact that I won't choose the next dog at all: someone will offer me a pup and I'll take it reflexively, whether it be another shorthair, a hunting cocker, or Chesapeake Bay retriever. There are people, to paraphrase, who are born to choose their dogs. Others have their dogs thrust upon them. I belong to the latter group.

Sam was thrust upon me by Vern, who called out of the blue one day to say he had a dog to give me, repayment for some favor my father had done for him long ago. The dog, Pee Wee, was just a year old, he said. Pee Wee had been returned by an indignant buyer who complained that the dog wouldn't gain weight, had an underbite, and, the final insult, his testicles were too small. Too small for what the man didn't say.

"He was kinda the runt of his litter," Vern admitted, but he'll make you a good little bird dog."

My previous "free hunting dog" was Betsy, a beautiful black and white springer spaniel from bench stock who, it quickly became apparent, had had all the nose and sense bred out of her in favor of flawless conformation and a lovely gait. Once she did actually blunder into a sitting rooster, which subsequently flushed and, to Betsy's horror, crashed dead to the ground in front of her when I shot. I found her a good home in the suburbs and vowed not to take any more free dogs. But when Vern called I had no money to spend on a pup and I wanted a hunting dog in the worst way. This dog, I told myself, would be different because Vern's shorthairs were proven hunters. I'd seen Peter Gunn tear up the field at NSTRA events and killed my first rooster over him, too. Besides, my wife, who believed her German shepherd was enough dog for the two of us, was conveniently out of town. What else could I say but yes?

I drove over to Vern's house the next day and he led me past pen after pen of lean, athletic shorthairs, tails cut long, their predominantly white coats suggesting more than a trace of English pointer somewhere in their bloodlines. Vern had sixty dogs at the time. Fifty-nine of them ran to the wire when he passed their pens, wagging their tails, sticking their noses through the mesh. One sat off in the background, barking suspiciously.

"That's the dog I had in mind for you," said Vern, pointing past the crowd around the fence to the bony little dog sitting against the back wall. Vern went into the pen, caught Pee Wee, and clipped a leash to his collar. The dog immediately pulled and strained as hard as he could, so Vern showed me how to loop the lead once around the dog's middle to keep him under control.

Out in the yard, Vern produced a fly rod with a pigeon wing on the line and flipped it in front of the dog. I'd seen him do this before with tiny young puppies, and had watched them lock into stylish points. Pee Wee dove on the wing and ripped it to shreds.

"Well," said Vern, yanking the tattered wing out of the dog's mouth and putting the rod away quickly, "that doesn't mean anything. Let's take him for a run."

I nodded, at a loss for words. We let Pee Wee loose in the field behind the house.

"Look at that tail," Vern murmured in admiration, as Pee Wee streaked for the horizon, "Straight up in the air. Now that's style."

How could he tell? The dog was already out of sight. He came tearing back into view moments later from an entirely different point of the compass, no doubt having just completed a quick circumnavigation of the globe. I'd never seen a dog this fast in my whole life.

"Will he retrieve ducks?" I asked.

"Nope," said Vern, "He's a bird dog."

"I'll take him," I heard myself saying. Here we go again, I thought.

Despite my reservations, I accepted Pee Wee with genuine gratitude; Vern's pups aren't cheap and the dog's papers were full of field trial champions. I loaded Pee Wee and a bag of dog food into the back of my Super Beetle, said goodbye, and there I was. I changed Pee Wee's name, which I hoped would raise his self-esteem, and bought a book on how to train pointing dogs.

What followed was disaster, frustration, and despair. One incident sums up our early hunts together. I was walking the bean field behind the house. Sam was tearing along as usual, happily bumping and chasing birds a couple of hundred yards ahead of me. Finally, I managed to catch his attention with the whistle and he swerved slightly in response. (I would whistle at Sam that year with the same vague hopefulness I feel when blowing a call at ducks. "Look, I've turned him!" I would sometimes exclaim to my long-suffering hunting companions in delighted surprise.) Just then a small plane flew over us, low, maybe five hundred feet off the ground.

Sam flashed me a look, almost a shrug that said, "Hey, I've got a plane to catch" and took off. He chased the plane across the huge expanse of plowed black earth until he was just a tiny white speck in the distance. I whistled and screamed myself hoarse. I was hoarse most of the time that fall.

The next year, I worked Sam on a checkcord all summer with marginal results. Off the cord, he would respond to the whistle at close range, but inevitably something in the distance would catch his eye and he'd bolt. As a countermeasure, I ordered a pair of rubber balls on nylon rope to hang from Sam's collar. These "Dog Compensators," the catalog copy explained, would slow the dog down by interrupting his gait and thwart his efforts to run big. Eagerly ripping open the package, I had the Dog Compensators snapped on Sam's collar while the UPS truck was still backing out the driveway. I watched with ill-concealed glee as he hobbled slowly around the house, confused by the nylon ropes tangling around his legs and the rubber balls bouncing off his shins. Incredible, I thought, almost lightheaded with euphoria and relief, my dog problems are solved for just four ninety-five, plus shipping and handling.

I should have known better. The first time I hunted Sam with the compensators on, he nearly caught a rabbit in a pure, straightaway footrace in an open field, the rubber balls streaming behind him like an aviator's silk scarf in an open cockpit.

A shock collar, purchased the next summer for considerably more than four ninety-five plus shipping and handling, finally brought Sam under control. There was, he soon came to realize, something out there that could hurt him and he started checking back, looking to me for protection. Our bond strengthened. My blood pressure lowered and my temper improved. Sam still ranged wide, but from then on I knew his wanderings would be roundtrips instead of one-way.

The electric collar served its purpose, but Sam became collar-wise, behaving in the field only if he wore the real collar or the dummy. I always felt as if I were cheating with the collar and that Sam was restrained rather than trained, so after the collar broke down one time too many, I sold it and bought a pair of track shoes. When Sam stopped responding to the whistle, I'd put on my running shoes and took him to a twenty-acre grassy field that was clipped so short there was no cover anywhere but along the fencelines. Sam liked to race down the fence and around the square, looking for birds.

I'd start him in one corner, whistling until I was satisfied he wasn't responding, then sprint diagonally across the field to cut him off at the far corner. If Sam paused to sniff around the locust tree, I could beat him to the brush pile near the old gate. Then I'd hide in the corn across the fence and leap out yelling when Sam arrived. He now believes I am faster than he is, which has done wonders for his obedience.

Other than the sprints, the collar work, yard work, and force-learning to retrieve, the rest of Sam's training consisted simply of turning him loose on wild birds before, after, and during the season. I may not have had any experience as a dog trainer myself, nor money to hire a pro, but I did have time to walk the dog every afternoon and there were wild pheasants on tap right across the road.

While my son was young enough to fit in a baby carrier, I'd strap him on my back almost every day from mid-July until mid-October and again from the end of the season in January until the hens began nesting in the spring. We'd follow Sam around the fields, letting the dog learn everything there was to know about pointing pheasants—when to creep, when to chase, how to push roosters hard without making them flush.

My dog remains far from perfect. He chases birds he flushes. The aggressiveness he's learned from pheasants carries over very poorly to woodcock; he crowds them and bumps as many as he points. He has a hard time picking up dead roosters because he invariably stands on one wing with both feet while trying to lift the body. He refuses to swim. Even today, at the dog middle age of eight, the sight of a pheasant flushing still sends a jolt of adrenaline to his brain that often renders him totally uncontrollable for several minutes afterwards. But the experience he gained in those seasons of working wild pheasants eight months a year, combined with a nose handed down from field trial champions, adds up to an uncanny talent for finding and pinning roosters.

During those afternoon runs, as I huffed along behind Sam with my son bouncing up and down and chortling in the backpack, I learned how to read my dog. Ever stylish, even joyous in the field, Sam's expressive body made it easy for me to understand what his nose was telling him about the hidden world of birds and scent beneath my feet. Soon I could read his every twitch the way an expert fisherman reads the slightest movement of his bobber.

Watching him track birds, I came to understand pheasants, too. When I hunted without a dog, I imagined pheasant hunting as a sort of walk through a minefield. Pheasants were hunkered down everywhere in the coverts, I assumed, heads pulled in like turtles, hoping you would walk past without noticing them. If you stepped close enough to a sitting bird, it would explode in your face with a disconcerting rattle of wings. When, after miles of tramping, a bird finally flushed at my feet, invariably I would repeat the dogless hunter's bromide to my companions: "We must have been walking by birds all day." I'd say it sagely, and my partners would nod in assent. Years later, with Sam's educated nose as my guide, I realized that pheasants slink, sprint, and double back, usually only sitting when trapped. If hunting with a dog increased the weight of my game bag, it also increased my respect for the wiles of pheasants.

As Sam has changed from liability to asset, and the Conservation Reserve Program has fueled a boom in pheasant populations, we've begun to enjoy the kind of success I'd always dreamed about. Where in previous years a three-bird limit was at best a biannual event, some days we're back home in little more than an hour after shooting our three birds over hard points. Other days there are long, satisfying chases through the CRP fields as Sam points and breaks over and over again on the trail of long-spurred, wise old roosters. I keep up as best as I can, breathless with exertion and anticipation both as Sam tiptoes after the birds and, more often than not, holds them until I arrive.

These latter outings invariably leave me drenched in sweat, and, by late November, I've usually shed a good ten pounds. Sam, always scrawny to begin with, looks positively cadaverous after a month of hard hunting. Effective predators, I'm well aware, must not only capture dinner, they must expend fewer calories in the chase than they gain from the kill in order to survive. By that measure, Sam and I would be doomed to quick starvation in the wild no matter how many birds we killed in a year, a thought which lends a certain wry perspective to our success in the field.

Two seasons ago, on the day after a blizzard had buried my place and the birds were sitting tight below the new-fallen snow, I caught myself taking a pheasant from Sam and stuffing it into my game bag with my right hand while signaling the dog to hunt up the next bird with the left. Any rooster pheasant, I have always maintained, is a trophy, and here I was cramming the bird into my vest without pausing to pay respects. We'd been hunting so much and killing birds so fast in the previous weeks that I realized I'd come to view a rooster as little more than one-third of a limit. Chastened, I took a break for a few days of deer hunting—which unfortunately counts as a nonconsumptive activity for me these days—before returning to the fields with Sam and my shotgun. The pheasants had grouped up into big, skittish late-season flocks while I was off sitting in trees, and they remained unapproachable until the last days of the season.

"That's what we get for feeling sorry for them," I told Sam on a mid-December day when the only pheasants we saw were tiny specks scaling off into the distance.

Our luck finally changed after Christmas, beginning on the drizzly afternoon I took Sam to hunt an eighty-acre CRP field a couple of miles from my house. I parked on the shoulder of the gravel road by the field's edge and at the sound of the truck door closing, pheasants poured out of the field, flying almost directly over the hood of the green Dodge pickup. One, two, three, four...at least four roosters in the gaggle of ten pheasants who'd survived this long by learning precisely what that metallic "clunk" meant.

I lifted Sam over the fence, then followed, loading the gun after I'd crossed. The sound of the breech closing over a pair of low-brass 6s was the last straw for one more tense rooster, who flushed out of range and followed the rest to the safety of the heavily posted cornfield across the road. The minute I put him down, Sam began snuffling through the grass where the pheasants had flushed.

"Sam," I said, "You're wasting your time. They're gone."

In answer, he locked on point, then broke and began trailing. In front of the dog I caught a glimpse of a black shape slinking in the direction of the fence we'd just climbed. I turned and ran back towards the fence myself, anticipating a wild flush. Now we had the bird trapped—the shorthair creeping in behind him, the open road to his front, me in easy gun range of his escape route if he didn't stop and crouch when he ran out of cover. The rooster flushed ahead of the dog, and I let him fly across the road and dropped him among the cornrows, then put one foot on the bottom strand of wire and pushed down so Sam could scoot back through the fence to make the retrieve.

This time the bird was duly admired, his feathers smoothed, the long tail carefully arranged to protrude from one side of the game bag, not merely for the benefit of passing road-hunters, but so he'd look as good hanging up in the kitchen as he'd taste on the dinner table. I gave Sam a hand signal. "Hunt 'em up." I said, pointing left. Sam went right. I put the whistle in my mouth to turn him, then let it drop back to my chest. Why make him come back? The rooster in the game bag was compelling evidence that Sam, as usual, had a better idea than did I as to where the birds were going to be.

"All right, all right, we'll do it your way," I said in affectionate, feigned resignation. Taking a few steps after him, I realized the sound of the bell had faded away; Sam had either crossed the county line or was pointing a bird nearby. I climbed to the top of a small rise, conditioned by years of frustration to scan the horizon for a small white dot coursing distant fencelines. What I saw instead was Sam locked on point, just below the crest of the rise. Breaking open the gun to make sure I'd reloaded, I walked down to join him, wondering if the bird he held in the brome grass for me was a rooster or a hen. I've known for a long time now that my job in the field is not to run the hunt but to carry the gun and see what happens. Most of all, Sam has taught me that wherever your dog leads, it pays to follow.

Geoffrey Norman is the author of eight books and numerous magazine articles, many of them on the outdoors. He grew up in panhandle Florida and southeast Alabama where he hunted quail and learned to appreciate the big running pointers and setters. He lives in Vermont where he hunts grouse and woodcock over dogs that stay much closer. For ten years, Norman hunted the grown-over orchards and the alder swamps with a fine-boned Brittany named "Molly." When he reached the age of fifty, however, Norman's old longings asserted themselves. He is now trailing a hard charging liver-and-white pointer by the name of J.E.B. Stuart. "If we don't find any grouse," Norman says, "then we'll go find us some Yankee railroad bridges to burn."

A DOG NAMED BERNIE

by Geoffrey Norman

Bunch of us were sitting around talking about dogs. Hunters like to do this when they aren't hunting...talk about dogs, that is. They tell dog epics in a way that I imagine isn't too very far from the way the ancient Greeks used to sit around and tell stories about their warrior heroes. In fact, if you had a strong, big running pointer and named him Hector, you could tell of his deeds in iambic pentameter.

Long ago, in the Wiregrass of Georgia
There lived a creature of stout heart
Firm on the point; steady to wing and shot...

Well, you get my drift and anyway, I digress. The conversation I have in mind was not about heroic deeds so much as the comic kind. The mood was Aristophanes more than Sophocles, don't you see. The subject was dogs that, while they wouldn't win any trophies at the field trials, sure knew how to leave 'em laughing. People who have never spent any time around field dogs probably don't believe that a dog can have a sense of humor. Anyone who has hunted much with dogs knows otherwise. Emphatically. Some dogs are just born clowns. They can hunt—some of them are real good, as a matter of fact—but they live for laughs.

"You know," one of the men at the table said, "I had an old black Lab, several years back. Male. Name of Mose. That old dog was like one of those comedians who makes a living bumping into things or falling down. Mose couldn't get out of his own way. Walked right through the screen door to our kitchen one time, just like it wasn't there. That dog drove my wife right straight up the wall."

"Some women are like that," one of the philosophers said. A medievalist, probably.

"Yeah," the tale teller continued, "but there were plenty of times when I felt the same way. The dog loved to hunt and he was good in a duck marsh. But he was the *clumsiest* dog.

"If we were in a blind together, and I opened a Thermos and poured a cup of coffee, then it was for certain that Mose would decide that was the time to get up and turn around and spill my coffee. I don't know how many times he knocked the Thermos out of my hand, right when I was pouring the first cup of the day. One time, he hit it hard enough to knock it clean out of the blind. And the thing was, no matter how mad you were, no matter how much you wanted that hot coffee, there was always something funny about it."

Everyone agreed that there is something comically redeeming about a clumsy dog.

"Probably," the teller went on, "old Mose put on his greatest performance with somebody else in the blind. Friend of mine came down to hunt and he just fell in love with that dog. I tried to tell him the dog was a little bit…oh, *unpredictable*. But he wasn't having any. Said he and Mose would make an unbeatable team. So I dropped them off at one blind, in the dark, and

went on around the marsh and set up in another blind. I was maybe two hundred yards away. I could hear my friend talking to Mose, telling him to 'sit' and 'stay.' Then it was quiet until the sun came up and the ducks came in.

"Now, Mose didn't cause any problems when the ducks were overhead. He was first class, that way. And after a couple of passes, six or seven mallards came into the decoys in front of my friend's blind. I heard him shoot. Heard the splash when the duck hit the water. Then I heard him say, kind of soft and confident, 'Okay, Mose. Fetch.'

"And then, the next thing I heard was him yelling like he'd been stabbed with a hot fork.

"'No, Mose. No. *Whoa*, Mose.'

"But it was too late. I heard the dog hit the water. A little later, I heard my friend say, sort of soft and mournful, 'Oh, no.'

"I shouted across the marsh, kind of nervous, 'What happened?'"

"'My *camera*,' my friend said.

"I figured Mose had knocked it off the ledge and into the mud, or something. So I hollered, 'How bad is it?'

"'I don't know,' my friend said. 'I'll let you know when Mose gets back.'

"Now, at first I had a hard time figuring what he was talking about but when he explained it later on, it all came clear. It seems like he'd carried this brand new, very expensive Nikon camera with a zoom lens to the blind in his bag. If I'd have seen it, I would have told him to leave it at home or get another dog.

"Anyway, when he got settled, he took the camera out of the bag and hung it from a peg, by the strap, so he could reach up and get it. Probably figured he was going to get a nice shot of Mose coming in with a retrieve.

"Well … what happened was, he downed that first duck and told Mose to fetch. Mose took off and put his head through the loop of that camera strap and kept right on going. Hit the water with that Nikon around his neck. Like I say, he was a good worker, so he just swam on out to where that mallard was floating and picked him up, then turned around and swam back in. Of course, my friend didn't have a camera when he *really* needed one. I'd have given anything for a picture of old Mose, coming out of the water with a drake mallard in his mouth and a Nikon camera hanging around his neck. My friend was laughing so hard he couldn't hunt. And it was his camera."

Everyone agreed that this was pretty good stuff. More to the point, nobody doubted the story. Of course the Lab had taken off out of the blind with a camera around its neck. That was *fated*, as the Greeks would have said, from the moment that fellow stepped into the duck blind carrying his camera.

"You know," one of the other men at the table said, "that's pretty tough about ruining that camera. But I had an old Chesapeake that did that to a car one time."

"Went into the water with a car around its neck?" Chesapeakes have a reputation for feats of strength but this was pushing it.

"Nah," the man said. "What I meant was he *ruined* a car, same as that Lab ruined a camera. But actually—now that I think on it—it was a *van*, not a car."

"Oh. Well in *that* case …"

"Yeah," the teller went on, undeterred. "It was a silver van. Belonged to Avis. Kind of a hard bunch, in my view.

"Anyway, three of us were using this van. Three men and one Chesapeake, name of Tiny. Dog was built like a linebacker. With a similar disposition. But he was a hunter. He'd been swimming in freezing cold water all morning, retrieving bluebills, and when we decided it was time to quit, he looked at us like he thought we were a bunch of wimps.

"It was lunchtime and we drove a couple of miles to a restaurant. We left the shotguns and everything else, including Tiny, in the van so we figured we didn't need to lock it. What we didn't count on was *Tiny* locking it. But he did. Every single door. When we came out of the restaurant there was Tiny, sitting in the front seat of the van, with all the doors locked, and the keys in the ignition.

"We were all still wearing our hunting clothes and when Tiny saw us, he must have decided it was time to go again. He got excited. So he started eating the van.

"He started with the dash, then he moved on to the steering wheel. When he finished there, he went after the upholstery. We kept trying to talk to him and calm him down but, like I say, Tiny was a linebacker and hard to reason with. Somebody finally said, 'Let's break a window while there's still something left of the car.'

"So, we took a big old rock and smashed the window on the driver's side and got inside. There wasn't much left. We turned the van in to the Avis people the next day and had a real hard time convincing them that one dog had done all that. I told the manager that if she would supply the car, Tiny would be glad to give her a demonstration. She didn't think that was funny. I figure she was probably a cat lover."

Everybody agreed that this was a pretty good story: dog tearing a van apart from the inside while a bunch of helpless men stood around pleading with the dog to spare the vehicle. Then one of the men who had been silent up to this point said, "I knew of a dog, one time, did something that will top that."

Oh?

"Yeah, this dog was a Lab. A chocolate. Fellow who owned him called the dog Yoo Hoo, after the drink, you know.

"Anyway, Yoo Hoo was like most Labs. He was a good-timer and he just couldn't stand to be left alone. The fellow who owned him—name was Paul—was kind of a soft touch and instead of leaving Yoo Hoo at home, by himself and sad, he'd let him ride around with him in his truck while he did his errands. The dog spent so much time in the truck that I believe Paul had him to where he could wear a seat belt and work the radio.

"Well, one day Paul has to go into town from the house, which is out on a country road, and he whistles up Yoo Hoo and puts him in the shotgun seat. Paul gets in on the driver's side and starts down the driveway. It's about a quarter of a mile to the road and halfway there, Paul remembers something.

"It's a narrow drive so he can't just turn around. And, since he doesn't want to back all the way to the house, he throws it in park and leaves Yoo Hoo in the truck, with the motor running, while he goes back to the house. Won't be but a minute, you see."

"Uh oh," one of the listeners said.

"Yeah buddy," the narrator answered. "That was just too much opportunity for a Lab. And Paul made it worse by answering the phone and doing a couple of other things so he wound up spending fifteen or twenty minutes in the house. Then he walked out the front door, strolled down the driveway, and discovered that this truck was gone.

"Now, his first thought was that somebody had stolen his truck. Which was bad enough. But what made it worse was that the thief had also gotten Yoo Hoo. What's running through Paul's mind is that you can always get another truck but he'll never be able to replace that Lab.

"He's standing there in the driveway, feeling terrible and just about to turn around and go back to the house and call the cops when he hears something. The sound of an engine, down in the woods off the high bank where he built his driveway. He walks over and looks down into the woods. There is a clear set of tracks running, oh, about two hundred yards out into the woods and at the end of the tracks, there is the pickup with Yoo Hoo at the wheel. Paul figured that the dog had spent so much time in the truck, watching him, that he knew about the gearshift and how it worked. He said that if the dog had just had an opposable thumb, he might have been able to get the truck down the driveway and gone on into town. Question was, what did he have in mind once he got there?"

· · · · ·

I listened to all these stories, and more, and I enjoyed them. But I didn't have much to contribute. My dogs have come from the pointing breeds and they are the stoics. Some pointing dogs will work until they literally drop. They generally don't have the time for stunts. The comics come from among the retrievers. Especially the Lab. Since the day I sat and listened to those stories, I have met a Lab whose legend would hold up whenever the tales of great comic deeds are told. His name is Bernie.

He comes from Cleveland and the breeder named him after the Brown's great quarterback, Bernie Kosar. The name fits the dog as perfectly as a stretch sock. You could never think of him as "Bernard." He is a "Bernie" if ever there was one.

Bernie is a big yellow Lab with the kind of easy amiability that you see in a lot of big men. When you are big you can come on gentle and nobody is likely to think it is because you are weak. I suppose Bernie can fight. I've seen him nicked up. But he is a party animal, not a fighter.

Bernie has a good nose and lots of drive. He is an excellent retriever both as a pickup dog off a mule wagon or out of a duck blind. But he seems to have sensed early in the game that he is not any better at this sort of basic, meat-and-potatoes dog work than a lot of other yellow Labs. And Bernie wanted to be thought of as special. He was not content with a future that consisted of hundreds of competent, straightforward retrieves. Bringing duck after duck and quail after quail to the hand of a moderately grateful master in return for a few 'attaboys' was not the sort of vision to stir Bernie's soul. He was after bigger things and like the starlet whose acting skills are no better than average but is determined to be a star, Bernie decided to make himself outrageous—to become a legend.

Nobody remembers Oscar Wilde for his poetry. Bernie is probably as good at sniffing out a freshly shot quail in the broomweed as Wilde was with verse. Maybe better. But an ordinary pickup doesn't really get Bernie's juices flowing and sometimes he will get down off the wagon and run right past the spot where the bird has fallen. He will then proceed to run the country while the handler yells at him and the shooters mumble under their breaths about ill-trained dogs, and the pointers, which are still on point, must be wondering why this bozo is allowed to get away with murder while they get whipped if they bust one lousy covey.

Bernie seems to know just exactly how long this sort of behavior will be tolerated before serious repercussions result. He does not want to be left in the kennel next time or whipped too hard, for that matter, this time. He'll take a whipping but he is no masochist.

So, just when patience has been stretched to the breaking point, Bernie will suddenly remember what he has been sent out to do. He will make a straight line back to where the bobwhite fell, sniff around in the grass, make a show of picking up the scent and trailing—even if the bird fell stone dead and never moved an inch—and then dash in the last ten feet and with the bird safely in his mouth, lift his head very high so

Waiting to Run
by Robert K. Abbett
Artwork courtesy of the artist and Wild Wings, Inc., Lake City, MN 55041

Stone Wall Brittany
by Robert K. Abbett
Artwork courtesy of the artist and Wild Wings, Inc., Lake City, MN 55041

everyone on the wagon or riding horseback can admire his form. Then, if this doesn't get results, Bernie will take a victory lap or two around the wagon before he brings the bird in to his handler.

A routine pickup is never really routine when Bernie is involved. He has a way of making the easy ones look hard.

Then, there are the hard ones. When Bernie has to trail a runner, he milks it for every ounce of drama. You'd think the bird was armed and dangerous. And, of course, once the chase has ended, Bernie takes a victory lap.

On an unorthodox retrieve, he is even better. I watched him go after a runner that had gone down a gopher hole to hide and I consider it one of Bernie's finest moments. Bernie put his head into the gopher hole, then his feet, then his entire body until only his hindquarters were above ground. He moved approximately a truckload of red clay to get at that bird.

"Seems like old Bernie would rather be a coal miner than a bird hunter," one of the shooters, watching the show from the mule wagon, said.

"I just hope he doesn't find a rattlesnake down there," another shooter said.

At about that time, Bernie emerged from his excavations with the bird in his mouth. He got a round of applause from everyone on the wagon and that just made his day.

While Bernie's technique on land is colorful, it is when he gets around water that his instinct for theater truly comes through.

Like most retrievers, Bernie quivers with anticipation when the ducks are coming in. In Bernie's case, I think it is something like stage fright. He knows he'll be on soon (provided the human does his rather humdrum part and shoots a duck or two) and for an artist, no matter how many times you have done it before, it is always opening night.

First thing that happens when a duck hits the water and a shooter says "fetch," is that Bernie *launches* himself like one of those NBA basketball players going for a dunk on the cover of *Sports Illustrated*. Bernie milks his entry into the water for everything it is worth. Usually, this means the shooter is soaked.

This dramatic entry is especially interesting when it is done from a canoe. Bernie goes about ninety pounds and if your canoe does not have a lot of wetted surface, you can go right over. Shotguns and all. But this is a minor thing up against the making of a legend.

Occasionally, this big splash is enough to satisfy the ham in Bernie and the remainder of the retrieve will follow the normal pattern. Bernie will swim out to the duck, pick it up in his mouth, swim back, and give the duck to the shooter. But this is no sure thing. It is not possible to know when the ham in Bernie will take over and he will decide that theatrics are somehow called for.

This can take the form of something that might be called "hide the duck," which is pretty much what it sounds like. There is, however, no way to convey, on paper and in mere words, the kind of passions this seemingly harmless game can inspire. You wouldn't think grown men could be forced to such rhetorical heights by the actions of a mere dog. Bernie seems to think that the objective of this game is to get someone to go in over his waders and about half the time, he is successful.

Bernie also likes another game which might be called "Where is the duck?" This game is best played when Bernie is taken to a blind and asked to retrieve a duck that he did not actually see fall. In those cases where the duck is floating out in the middle of open water, plainly visible to all, Bernie might just swim past it, so close that the duck is swamped by his wake. Hunters on shore will scream things like, "Right there, Bernie. Right there."

Bernie will then begin to circle. First the circles will grow wider. Then, as the screaming of the hunters grows louder and more shrill, the circles will grow tighter and tighter, with the duck in the precise center like the ten ring on a target. Finally, Bernie will locate the duck and return to shore in triumph.

A variation on this one occurs when the duck has fallen someplace where he can't been seen from shore. Say, in a patch of cattails. In a case like this, when Bernie is told to "fetch," he responds with a look and something like a shrug as though to say, "Fetch *what?*"

You can point as urgently as Napoleon directing his men through the Alps and Bernie will continue to give you the look. Finally, you decide to throw something out in the area where the duck has fallen. Then, of course, Bernie leaps into action. Big leap, lots of water splashed back on everyone on shore.

The basic comic script, here, calls for the dog to swim out and pick up the stick that the hunter has thrown to mark the duck. Bernie does this with the best of them. But he also seems to realize that this is pretty humdrum, pie-in-the-face sort of stuff. That what it needs is a *twist*.

Bernie has come up with a couple of variations on this theme and is, no doubt, working on others. The first variation calls for Bernie to swim right past the duck and even bump into it on his way to fetch the stick. He can do this with an absolutely straight face so that the hunter can believe that Bernie was actually unaware the duck was even there. Bernie's expression does not change even when three or four hunters scream, in unison, *Right there*. The deadpan is worthy of Johnny Carson.

A second, more elaborate variation calls for Bernie to swim out where the stick has fallen close to the duck. He ignores the stick, picks up the duck, and turns back for the shore where the chorus is chanting *Good boy, thataway Bernie, bring him here*. About half way back to shore, Bernie drops the duck, turns around and picks up the stick which he then brings to shore. It is as though Bernie wants everyone to understand that while he certainly knows the difference between a duck and a stick, he is not going to be locked into some rigid, orthodox thinking according to which a duck is *always* preferable to a stick. Some days, you see, he just feels more like retrieving sticks, even if there is a duck around.

It was on the day when I first saw this performance that I decided Bernie was interested, above all, in creating a legend. Now, while Bernie is certainly a ham, he is not necessarily a *prima Donahue*. He will jump—literally—at the opportunity to share the stage with other actors, though it is better if they are not dogs. He seems, in fact, to prefer beaver.

Take Bernie up to a quiet, concealed pond in the hour before dawn and everything will be fine unless he hears the slap of a beaver tail. Then he is off. Swimming, diving, running, and barking. Just putting on a hell of a show which, in turn, inspires the beaver.

Usually beaver are pretty dour and phlegmatic. No time for fun and games as long as there is an undammed stream or an ungirdled aspen tree anywhere on the planet. But when Bernie comes around, beaver seem to turn into good-time-Charlies and hell-raisers with nothing to do but swim around the pond slapping the water with their tails. Near as I can tell, the game has a lot in common with tag and Bernie is always "it." One thing is certain, no duck has ever been inclined to join in the fun, so on those mornings when Bernie and the beaver are at play, you have to be content to watch them and forget the hunt.

Bernie will also chase a deer or a turkey. Get close to a porcupine or a skunk. He is just naturally gregarious that way. He will run with just about anything that is alive and roll in just about anything that is dead. While he doesn't exactly play with insects, he will eat them. I've seen him wake up from a dead sleep to nail a grasshopper on the wing, which was not half as funny as the time he chomped down on a hornet that happened to fly by.

Bernie eats lots of interesting things, including some that were meant to be dinner. He has been thrown out of a lot of kitchens. Once, when he was inadvertently left in one where there was a ham on the counter, he managed to knock over a planter, open a faucet, and turn on a blender in his attempt (successful) to get at that meat. He spent several days in a maximum security kennel after that. Most dogs would have gotten life but Bernie always seems able to wrangle a pardon.

Part of the reason is that he is always glad to see you. Genuinely glad. Bernie does not have to be called. If you are a kid, he is always ready to play. It would take three ten-year-olds, working in shifts, to wear him out. Kids have pulled his tail, stuck fingers in his eyes, and generally abused him, but he has never raised his voice or shown anyone his teeth. Bernie will go anywhere and do anything for kicks so it doesn't seem so terrible if he can't be relied upon to stay with the script. He is an improviser and a comic. Aristotle, who could appreciate the Greek epics as well as anyone, wrote that man is the only animal that laughs. Which may be. I'm not going to argue with Aristotle.

But he never knew Bernie. And while I've never actually seen Bernie laugh, I know that he is a comic and that if nothing else, he lives for the laughter of others. There is just no other way to account for him.

Tom Huggler has had an ongoing love affair with dogs for most of his forty-eight years and cannot imagine hunting without at least one four-footed partner leading the way. He currently owns two English setters, a shorthair, and a golden retriever and wants to get a yellow Lab to fill the void recently created when Holly, the long-time companion described in this story, passed on to hunt in other places. "A heaven for hunting dogs?" Huggler asks. "Why not? An animal that asks so little and brings us so much pleasure surely lives on in another time and place." A full-time freelance writer and author of ten books, Huggler, who lives near Lansing, Michigan, is Hunting Dogs columnist for North American Hunter magazine.

OWNED AND DISOWNED BY HUNTING DOGS

by Tom Huggler

According to my mother, who keeps track of such things, by the time I left home at nineteen, a total of thirty eight dogs had passed through our family of three boys. Some of the dogs actually hunted. I'm forty-eight now and can only guess at how many four-footed partners have shared a finger-fed portion of my lunches served in duck blinds and on truck tailgates. Some of these charges hunted, too, and all are memorable. I have owned and been owned by beagles and Brittanies and goldens and Labs and many doe-eyed English setters—my Achilles heel, to be sure— but I am equally impressed by pointers, retrievers, flushers, and trackers who have a nose for game and are true to the law of their blood.

Let me tell you about some of them.

The hunting instincts are immeasurably strong in certain individuals and within some breeds. For example, although I've never owned one, springer spaniels score high in the sheer guts department. Somewhere in a file I have a black-and-white photo of a bouncy springer named Brandy climbing a barbed-wire fence to get to a South Dakota ring-necked pheasant on the other side. Another spaniel named Molly, an old fat female that looked like a brown-and-white barrel with legs, hadn't hunted in years when she insisted on tagging along one day on our Iowa pheasant hunt. "Let her go with you," the farmer-host hollered across the field when I tried to coax the disobedient dog back to the barnyard. "It'll be good for her."

Snorting and panting all day, Molly tried to keep up with my friends and me and our younger dogs. We got to feeling sorry for her and began waiting for the game old gal to catch up. Groaning, two of us hiked the heavy dog up and over fences. Exhausted from that and miles of tramping, at day's end we stumbled over our long shadows back to the farm with Molly in tow. She barely made it to her doghouse. Next year when we returned I asked the farmer how she was.

"Molly? That hunt was her last hurrah. She died a couple of days later."

A friend of mine once lost a $5,000 champion beagle when the dog literally ran itself to death chasing snowshoe hares in Michigan's Upper Peninsula. In Oklahoma I let a wobble-legged, half-blind English pointer named Sam find a downed bobwhite within my reaching distance. Closing his eyes, Sam gummed the bird awhile, savoring what turned out to be the season's last retrieve. In Colorado, three of us held down a young German shorthaired bitch and removed a faceful of porcupine quills. An hour later she pointed and retrieved her first sage grouse. Such dogs never fail to inspire.

Some of the best ones are tightly meshed to their owners. Sam and his son Jake, a pair of Chessies owned by Bill Wood of Bismarck, rarely took their eyes off Bill the whole day we hunted the North Dakota prairie. Later, Jake held a sharp-tailed grouse for the camera until Bill told him he could open his aching jaws.

A drahthaar owned by Iowan Miles Trachel was in the act of killing my young setter who had nosed the bigger dog's fanny until Miles—and only he could have done it—shocked his dog off the doomed pup. One day on Michigan's Saginaw Bay I watched a 110-pound yellow Lab named John break his tether in our blind, leap into the icy water, and challenge dangerous

four-foot waves. John wanted to help his owner, who was bouncing around in our small boat, to retrieve a goldeneye a half-mile out into the heaving bay. I wondered if John's heart would burst before he made it back to safety.

For years I have hunted small game and upland birds all over North America in the company of dogs like these and others. I am not a professional trainer or breeder although I have managed to fumble both and still put an occasional star in my kennel over the last thirty years. When good dogs find game, it provides a prologue to the exciting drama of flush or run, swing and shoot, hit or miss, and I live for such hair-trigger tension. But I am familiar with the heartburn that even good dogs produce when they screw up. I know, too, about the heartache all dogs cause when they grow old, are stolen, or die.

Dogless hunters do not make a habit of burying their partners. There is a reason why hunting dogs don't live very long, but I do not know what the reason is. I just know that five years or so, which is the average length of time that canine maturity and experience transect with prime age, is far too short a time.

A Kansas friend of mine, who hunts with Labrador retrievers and who is smarter than I, figured this out many years ago. So whenever his youngest dog turns five, he starts over with a puppy. The last time we walked native prairie together, his Labs were aged twelve, seven, and two. For him, the inevitable changing of the guard is always predictable and much less painful than trying to fill a void with emptiness.

Smelt-Eating Beagle

Memories help me to fill the void. When I was growing up, my dad kenneled his bird dogs, retrievers, and hounds in the backyard where Mother could tolerate them, even feed them when we boys forgot. Most of these dogs were mutts, their ancestry usually questionable, their working ability often as faulty as the guns and hunting gear that Dad had traded for them. A .35 Remington deer rifle with cracked scope was appropriate dicker bait for a retriever with a steel trap for a mouth.

And so on. One of these backdoor deals was a beagle pup Dad brought home one day in the pocket of his deer-hunting coat.

Our father steadfastly called the dog "Emil," but to my brothers and me he was always "Boots." No matter; he rarely came by either name. Emil/Boots turned into one of the most unusual dogs I ever knew, even though he spent only a few years with us before becoming a highway traffic statistic.

I was about twelve at the time when I first saw the tri-colored puppy with the impish face peering out from the woolen depths of my father's coat. Placed on the kitchen linoleum, the pup scampered off, his white forelegs prancing like a drum major in white boots.

"Let's call him Boots," Dave, my older brother, said.

"I like Emil," Dad said without explaining why, and then, upon discovering a spreading wet spot in his coat pocket, offered several other names for the newest arrival in our home.

I pause briefly to explain that, although my father loved most pets (especially dogs), they rarely returned the sentiment. Another time he brought home a cardboard box containing a crippled pigeon he had rescued from the roof of a house where he had been installing a television antenna. As Dad sat down to a late supper of spaghetti, he told us boys there was a surprise in the box. We tore it open, and the pigeon flew straight to my father's balding head where it perched just long enough to relieve itself. As I was saying, Dad received little respect from pets, wild or domestic.

The problem was that he had little patience with them. Dad simply expected his hunting dogs to mind and hunt for him, regardless of whether they had been trained to do so. My father met his match with Boots, who was stubborn and completely unafraid of anything. With the right trainer Boots might have turned into a crackerjack hound because he was an excellent cold tracker. But the critters he tracked were not always rabbits and hares. I remember hearing him plodding through the loose snow of a northern Michigan swamp and cutting loose with squeals and an occasional bawl as he puzzled out a snowshoe hare track. Suddenly the swamp would go silent. Then the hound's voice would take on a machine-gun attack—sign of a jumped deer.

If we could get to Boots soon enough, we could pull him off the track. If not, the chase could involve hours and miles. Once Boots was caught, Dad would wail on him a while, put him back down in a new cedar swamp, and twenty minutes later the beagle would sing off louder than before on another deer track. Boots grew to expect the swift and certain punishment, yet he always returned to his deer-running ways.

I never knew a hunting dog to have more moxie. One time we drove to the farmland country to hunt pheasants. Tooling down a rural road in our '57 Chevy, Dad pulled up next to a farmer walking a beautiful Irish setter. I was sitting in the back seat with Boots on my lap while the men talked through the open window.

"Sure, you can hunt," the farmer was saying, and about that time Big Red put his paws on the window for a look inside. In a flash of brown and white, and without even a warning growl, Boots leaped for the interloper's throat. The red dog fell on his back with the crazed beagle all over him, shaking his head like a pup with a huge stuffed toy. Had he fought back, the bigger dog could have bitten Boots in two. Instead, the farmer kicked the beagle off his prize setter while Dad got a finger in Boots's collar.

It took a long time to find another place to hunt that day.

On the subject of former dogs, most hunters think back to golden afternoons replete with head-high setters on point, perfect retrieves, game-heavy hunting coats. When my mind wanders to Boots, I remember cold nights driving two-track roads looking for a worn-out hound, the rush of cold air mixed with the acrid fumes from my father's ever-present Phillip Morris, embarrassment mixed with worry, an empty game pouch—and smelt. Yes, smelt. Boots loved them. I recall one spring evening when I was sixteen or so, I stood at the kitchen sink cleaning smelt for my supper. Only Boots and I were home, and I well remember the hopeful expression on that otherwise mischievous face every time I lifted one of the little fish from an iron skillet on the stove.

I ate one, then tossed him one. It disappeared in a tongue flick, only to be replaced by that expectant look. One for me, one for Boots. Pretty soon the skillet was empty, so I fried another batch. After about twenty fish each, I began to wonder if the beagle could eat more than I. Two hours later we had consumed fifty smelt each, and I looked at my tummy with unease and a little shame. Boots's stomach was slung like a well-fed lion, and a glassy look was fast replacing the eager glint in his eyes.

He must have known he had me because I could barely swallow number fifty-one and stopped halfway through fifty-two. Meanwhile, Boots lay on his side and slowly chewed, his belly curved like a scimitar and taut as a drum. The tail of smelt number fifty-two disappeared. When he nibbled on number fifty-three, I declared him the world champion.

To this day, I do not like smelt, but I suspect that Boots still does. I figure he gets a platter now and then, too, soon after working up a good appetite from chasing deer.

Somewhere on Point

English setters gobble more ground in less time than any other breed of bird hunter. The brain, or maybe it is blood genetics, tell the dog to run hard and run long. Those that are mostly white in color float like elegant spirits over prairie grass and flash through aspen slashings. But their first points are puppy clumsy: the legs misshapen, the body corkscrewed. You can mold such a young dog on point as though she is Play Dough in your hands. "Cock that foreleg now. Keep the head up. Up, up. That's it, girl." You will also not resist closing fingers around and stroking that magnificent tail. Like the feather plume on a musketeer's hat, it must be carried proudly high.

I played with setters long before I understood these things, certainly before I was old enough to hunt, with a gun at least, behind them. The first was a family dog named Queenie, a big out-of-control runner. Queenie was bold, knot-headed, unmanageable in the way that only setters can be, but I suppose that was mostly my fault. On autumn afternoons when the elementary school bus deposited me in front of our rural home, I'd race to change clothes and unleash the excited dog. Then we'd head for the big fields beyond our lawn. We knew our roles well: Queenie's was to chase the pheasants; mine was to chase Queenie.

I remember one time when she slammed, unexpectedly, into a pose as rigid as the cement lion on our front porch. She had been racing, pink tongue to the wheat stubble. Suddenly, it was as though she struck an invisible wall. Her body flag flew up and somehow she managed a pretzel bend to stare back over her front shoulder at me, or so I thought until I approached close enough to see she was mesmerized by a pile of old cornstalks. The pile ignited, and a big cockbird, all on fire, came roaring out.

That day I fell in love with English setters. I was six, maybe seven, years old.

Queenie's last big run occurred a couple of years later when a farmer shot her for trespassing. That is what our family was told, anyway, but never could prove.

When you are grown, you learn to savor life more than during the younger years, or realize you are a fool if you cannot. Perhaps better than most, hunting dog owners know how time always compresses rather than expands. A dog can be born, grow up, and die in the span it takes some people to earn a college degree. The eight years I owned a remarkable setter named Lady Macbeth seemed to pass with the mere snap of fingers.

I am holding a photographic slide of her now, and she is on point. Foreleg cocked, nose haughty and high, it is a classic setter pose, one that Robert Abbett would drool for. The poignancy of Macbeth's points—a certain compactness of energy, a stick-pinned sharpness—always reminds me of a drawn bow. The bracken fern blurs under the ghostly birch, and I swear I can smell the new richness of decaying woods through the celluoid. May it always be that way.

Her death was completely unexpected and remains a mystery today, years later. I found her, dead, in the kennel at feeding time one evening. There were no signs of suffering. I could not bury her on the farm where she was born because I had to leave for a long trip the next morning, and there was an autopsy to do. The autopsy proved nothing.

Those are the facts. They are the easy part to explain.

The evening before, we played on the back lawn and she pretended there were birds hiding under the roses, just blooming. Macbeth's tail chased her nose, wormlike, as though the hunting was for real. When I told her about our plans for the fall, she made that silly grin again. Our travels would take us to many places in search of native grouse. Some of these, such as blue grouse and ptarmigan, Macbeth had never seen. But I was confident that she could handle them, like she had learned to hunt Mearns quail and mountain quail and other game birds on other trips. She was confident, too.

At first, I thought about canceling the grouse journey. What was the purpose, I asked myself, if I could not take along the partner that had shared so much with me in the past?

Now I sort through other stacks of slides, and in my mind's eye I recall other things worth remembering. Scenes when Macbeth would retrieve birds that I was unable to get to—a pheasant that died in the middle of a duck pond, a grouse that fell into shirt-shredding tangle. The day she learned to hunt brushy fencerows for bobwhites by vacuum cleaning them toward me. Her first taste of prairie grouse in Nebraska. How frustrated she grew when scaled quail tried to sprint from New Mexico into Arizona.

I remember other things that were irritating or humorous but are part of any partnership, too. Her general bitchiness with other dogs and sometimes children as she grew older. Her refusal to eat the supper I prepared in a hub cap, pried loose from my Chevy pickup, because I had forgotten her regular dish. The evening in the baggage terminal at Chicago's O'Hare Airport when she barked the instant she recognized me.

Progeny of a field trial mother and a gun dog father, Macbeth's permanence in my kennel was a fluke of sorts. By telephone, I had sold her as a pup to a friend from Kansas, after selecting a male for myself from the litter I was raising. I had her vet's certificate in hand and a reserved spot on an airplane leaving the next day. It is not fair to ship a nameless dog as though the dog was baggage, and so for want of a better name, I called her Ron's Star Point. That night the phone rang. It was Ron.

"I can't take the dog, after all," he said. "My wife left me this morning, and I don't know what I'm going to do. But I know it would be dumb for me to invest in a dog now."

So I kept Point, changing her name when an editor and hunting companion sent a letter telling me of his own new setter, Shakespeare. "You can't get any more English than that," he wrote. "Can you?"

The best dogs are those that form a special bond with their owners. I do not know how to explain that simply except to say that Macbeth and I had such a bond. There were times when I believe she could read my mind, and there is no doubt that I could read hers. She had ways of letting me know if she was happy or not, like the day when I came home from a sharptail hunting trip in North Dakota. I had not taken Macbeth because it was a short trip, and a sudden blast of frigid weather had me concerned about her safety in the cold belly of a DC-10.

I arrived in Michigan on a Sunday afternoon in early November with just enough time for a woodcock hunt in some local coverts. After being able to see forty miles on the treeless Dakota plains, it seemed strange to be tramping through aspen bamboo where I could see only forty feet. Also strange was the behavior of my dog. She ran off to hunt on her own, flushed wild, and refused to retrieve the only bird I shot. I was so mad I could taste copper. I hauled Macbeth into the truck and drove home. "I did this for you, fool!" I scolded. My dog squirmed into her corner of the truck and refused to meet my glare.

Soon, I softened and held out the warm hand of truce. Macbeth craned her pretty white head, sniffed my trousers, twisted her nose, and shrank back to her corner. Only then did I realize I still carried the odors of Dakota prairie and grouse along with the smells of strange dogs whose names I had already forgotten. I washed the clothing before we hunted again.

Macbeth could be headstrong, sure, but only to the degree that you hope for in a bird dog. A dog that does not test the obedience limits once in a while is not worth putting your name on its collar. I shot my last grouse over her on the last day of the calendar year, the final preserve pheasant in early February. I was proud of her both times, and I think she approved of my shooting.

No matter how open or tight the cover, a pointing dog *has to check in*. Unless I had done something to annoy her, Macbeth always checked in. Except when she was on point, and then it was up to me to find her.

Maybe you know. Maybe you, too, remember a time in southwest Kansas when a thirty-knot wind tried to unbutton your hunting coat. The wires between you hunters and your quail dogs were certainly down that day. First Mike lost his golden retriever for a frantic twenty minutes. Then it was Macbeth's turn to disappear. You watched her chase the busted covey she had overrun from the upwind side. Embarrassed, she ran two errant birds downwind for a quarter-mile, finally vanishing as a white speck over a little rise in the cut field of grain. You waited three minutes. Five minutes. No dog.

Remember how the tension mounted, along with your anger? "Excuse me," you tell your hunting partners. "I have a dog to punish."

But you should be the one spanked for not trusting your dog. There she is, locked up, another four hundred yards farther on! The wind stirs her tail feathering. You feel foolish and you apologize to your dog as you creep into shooting position, while she admonishes you with those nervous setter eyes. They dart from you to the bird and you know what she is thinking. "For God's sake, Thomas, where the hell have you been? Here's the quail, right under this milo stalk."

You kill the bird, a young cock, for your dog on a crossing shot. Her perfect retrieve means she has forgiven you. The law allows two more; instead you unload your gun. You have learned that when the cup will hold no more, it is time to stop trying to fill it.

And so that is how you will come to accept the loss of this dog, your favorite hunting partner. You had her at her absolute best, and, in spite of your many mistakes, you were also the instrument for some of her success. You know she was not great, at least not in the way the experts grade hunting dogs, but she was better than good and she made *your* Bird Dog Hall of Fame. Nothing else matters.

It is now several more autumns that you have walked those mountain saddles and aspen whips and windswept plains without her. There have been other dogs and other hunters, and sometimes you have walked alone. But not too often because you find yourself looking for a white setter with black speckling to check back with you. She was right here, wasn't she? and only a moment ago.

When she does not return, you realize she is on point somewhere else. You just have not found her, yet.

The Price

Some dogs do not cut it, in spite of their good looks and great breeding. They have to go, but getting rid of them is never easy. I'm talking about dogs whose synapses are short-circuited because of an aberrant gene or the way they were raised. You know, the old heredity versus environment thing that every parent agonizes over.

A few years ago I sold a setter puppy to an artist friend who fell in love with the litter runt. "Cleo," as we called her because of her gorgeous eyes circled with black, was the most handsome of the ten puppies. She was also an aggressive little bitch who harassed her litter mates and often bit the hands that fed her. I told my friend, who had a family of his own and had never owned setters, that Cleo was the worst possible choice. When he insisted on buying her, I refused to take his money. "Send me a check in a week," I said as he backed out of my driveway, the little furball wriggling like live macaroni in the arms of my friend's five-year-old son.

Two days later my friend was back in the driveway. Leaving the engine running and the door open, he thrust a cage with Cleo in it at me. "Here's your dog back," he blurted. "My kid has been bitten and scratched all to hell."

What do you do with a dog like that? Knock 'em in the head? I, for one, cannot, and so I traded Cleo for two fifty-pound bags of Purina. Then I gave away her mother—a tightly wired ground gobbler who had trouble hearing commands unless you first melted the wax in her ears with electricity—to an enormous Sicilian from Detroit who said he was one of boxer Thomas Hearns' bodyguards. I believed him.

You never know for sure what you will get from breeding (or buying). How can you tell, for example, if behind those liquid brown eyes there is functional gray matter? And once you commit yourself to any hunting dog that will not or cannot measure up, at what point do you disconnect and then dispose of the flunky? This much I know: The older I become, the less time I have to waste with dogs that are incorrigible or crazy. I would add "stupid" except I have never owned a dog that was flat-out dumb. Happy in his own ignorance, perhaps, like Odie in the Garfield comic strip, but never dim-witted to the point that the dog had not probed for my weaknesses and then figured out how to capitalize on them.

Such was a powerful, strong-willed male named Chaucer who was a guest in my kennel six years too long, which was also his age when I gave him away. Chaucer had more lives than a cat, and I suspect he is still alive today but do not know for sure.

I got him as a pup in March and all spring and summer we worked with a fly rod and wing, leash, and check cord. By the end of August, he appeared to be ready. Like an optimistic football coach, I broke training camp thinking I had a promising rookie on my team. Things began to fall apart soon after. In early September, when Chaucer was nine months old, he nearly died from a virulent disease. Upon returning home from a fishing trip, I found him in the kennel, lying on his side and covered with flies. He was barely breathing. I rushed Chaucer to the veterinarian, who gave him a shot of cortisone and put him on a drip diet of glucose. The next day the lab report came back: canine parvovirus. It was amazing that Chaucer lived at all, and several weeks passed before his health returned.

So the youngster missed his first hunting season, a critical experience in the life of any gun dog. Late the following summer, I sent him for professional training. "He's a different one," the trainer admitted when I came to pick up the dog. "He's either too willful or not too smart. It's hard to say for sure, but he sure as hell has a mind of his own. He lacks consistency, but I think he'll be okay if you hunt him a lot."

Instead, I spent most of Chaucer's second autumn in Alaska, and he did not get the field work he needed. Even so, I was not overly concerned because many male setters are notoriously slow to develop. So in the fall of 1985, when Chaucer was three, I took him and the other dogs on a three-month, cross-country odyssey to hunt quail. His problems became manifest on that trip.

Because Chaucer was socially ignorant, he behaved shabbily. He picked fights, for instance, with my friends' dogs—until a tough old Labrador changed his mind in Kansas. In Iowa, Chaucer pissed on the pant leg of my host and bared his teeth and growled whenever anyone tried to take a bird away from him. He refused to load in the trailer I pulled behind my motorhome unless I exhausted him first by "roading" him for miles. That wasted a lot of time because Chaucer was the strongest dog I had ever owned and he did not tire easily. About this time I took to calling him "Lunchmeat" and decided to give him away to the next farmer who commented on his handsome black eye patch.

Then Lunchmeat did something remarkable. In Oklahoma, he began to hunt birds instead of chasing deer into Texas. By the time we got to Missouri, he was holding bobwhites with some consistency. He backed Macbeth a time or two and even retrieved an occasional half quail after biting the birds in two to make sure they were dead.

In Arizona, Chaucer turned jerk again when he showed more interest in chasing jackrabbits than in finding Gambel quail. Arizona was also where he experienced how painful cholla can be. The other dogs quickly learned to avoid the prickly cactus, but Chaucer not only tangled with the miserable stuff, he bit at it. I spent half of one afternoon pulling spines from his face, palate, and testicles. One barb was completely through his tongue.

Then in New Mexico, Chaucer fell from an old pickup as we lumbered over corrugated roads at 45 mph. Floyd, my friend who was driving, stopped when he noticed the tailgate had banged open. There were our dogs, sensibly lying away from danger near the cab. All except Chaucer. He was gone.

"Good God!" Floyd said. "He must have fallen out. Where do you suppose he is?"

Five minutes later, we spotted a small dust funnel on the horizon. Borrowing Floyd's binoculars, I could make out my dog, galloping toward us, his pink tongue nearly touching the dry roadbed.

"In forty years of hunting, I've never had a dog fall out of a truck," Floyd said. "No wonder you call him Lunchmeat."

The next year Chaucer had good days and poor days afield. Meanwhile, like a good cabernet Macbeth steadily improved, and so I began to rely even more on her, leaving Chaucer in the dog box of my trailer.

"For pete's sake get rid of him," advised my friends, some of whom are experts on dogs.

I could not bring myself to do it.

Each year before bird season, I run my dogs, one at a time, on a leash alongside the truck. I do this in the cool evenings, along back roads where there is little traffic. The dogs love the exercise. One evening after Chaucer had enjoyed his turn during a two-mile romp, I removed the leash and told him, "Kennel up." He wrinkled a lip in the manner of a snot-nosed sixth grader headed for the principal's office. Could Chaucer have spoken, he might have said, "Kennel up yourself, sucker." Angry, I tried to grab his collar. He scooted backwards, into the other lane and a LeSabre that happened to be roaring by.

If you have ever witnessed an auto accident, you know the sinking feeling when time stops. The low-slung car dragged my dog a long way before it shuddered to a stop and the dust cleared and I could see. There lay Chaucer, misshappen and in certain pain, although he neither yelped nor howled. Two thoughts raced through me: (1) It's over for him, (2) Thank God it wasn't Macbeth. I told the lady driver, who was shaken over hitting her first animal, that it was not her fault and to go home. Then I tried to figure out what to do with my suffering dog.

I could hardly believe he was still alive. I knew he had a broken back and would bite me if I tried to move him. Bending over the stricken dog, I talked gently; amazingly he seemed to know who I was. A plan evolved. My vet lived only a couple of miles away. I would knock on a nearby door, call the doctor, and ask him to come quickly and give Chaucer a mercy needle. But as I walked across the road back to the truck, I was shocked when my dog began dragging himself after me. As gently as possible, I muzzled him with a handkerchief, then found another and daubed at the blood oozing from a nasty gash to his head. He was bleeding through his nose and mouth and his undersides were scraped raw. Carefully I loaded Chaucer into the truck and drove to the vet's office.

I told you this dog had more lives than a cat. The doctor found no broken bones, just severe lacerations and a probable concussion. "We'll keep him here for a couple days," he said. "He may come out of this with just a big headache."

Chaucer healed fast. Two weeks later I took him to Michigan's Upper Peninsula for my annual grouse hunting camp. He thanked me by running off the first time I slipped his leash in a promising cover. Two hours later I found, and punished, my dog. Two weeks after that was the last time I took him hunting.

It was a balmy October afternoon when three friends and I chanced upon a heavy flight of woodcock. The poplar slashings were stiff with birds, and we were getting the kind of gunning that can carry a man through the long winter. Unfortunately, Chaucer had run off on his own adventures earlier in the day and was now missing all the fun—bittersweet action for me because I was furious over my dog's antics. I looked for him until dark, then left a hat in the woods in case he came back. He didn't. I drove home two hundred miles, my neck throbbing from tension. The next day the phone rang. A friend of a friend had found the errant Chaucer—six miles from where I had last seen him—and my name and telephone number on his collar.

"What do you want me to do with him?" Kevin, my friend, asked over the telephone.

I did not hesitate. "Give him away."

"He's a beautiful dog, but I don't think anyone wants him," Kevin said. "Hunting season is about over. But the guy who found him says he'll take him to the pound for you."

I know now how a mother feels when her good-for-nothing son is hauled downtown for questioning. Or a wife tells a skirt-chasing husband goodbye and this time means it.

"Do it," I said and slept well that night.

But two days later, there was a knock at the door. It was Kevin, and in his car was Chaucer, bounding from the back seat to the front seat and back again, happy to be home once more.

"They couldn't turn him in," Kevin explained. "The dog is just too...How do you say it?...a born loser, I guess. You can't put down a dog like that. He has a way of looking at you. It's in his eyes."

"I know."

It was Chaucer's last big roundup. For the next several months he stayed in his chainlink kennel, like a convict, except for brief bouts of exercise in the yard of my farm while I prepared food and changed his water. Sometimes I would take him to the office where he liked to sleep under the desk while I wrote. I stopped calling him Lunchmeat because he never again got the chance to do anything wrong. The following spring I gave him to a young married couple who wanted a pet.

It is the price one sometimes pays for owning bird dogs.

The Problem with Holly

The problem with Holly is that she is growing old much too fast and may not make it to grouse hunting camp next October. At night my wife and I pill the yellow Labrador with Ascriptin, and Holly whimpers when I massage her arthritic hips too hard. Her wheezing reminds me of an old switch engine slowly chugging through the woods. Her eyes have developed the smoky, opaque look of a glass marble that is flawed. This, I feared, was cataracts but is advancing age—according to her vet—and perfectly normal.

I am the one not normal. At nearly thirteen years of age Holly is the oldest hunting dog I have ever owned, and I am writing about her now because I do not have any experience here and am reasonably certain I will fumble the words later. Whoever said we should pay our tribute to the living, not the dead, was right, and the truth is I owe this dog more than I can tell you in a few short paragraphs.

By now, you know that I have an immense soft spot for English setters. The irony is that over many years I have spent thousands buying and training setters only to have them die in their prime, run off, get stolen, sold at loss, or turn into absolute rascals. Holly cost me seventy-five dollars when I bought her in 1980 from a Mayville, Michigan, breeder. I needed a meat-and-potatoes hunter, a clean-up partner to fetch ducks and to rout pheasants from the places the racing setters missed. Training? I spent twenty bucks to enroll Holly in a dog obedience class at the local high school. I admit to being surprised when she took first place, beating out a thousand-dollar golden with the improbable name of Octavius.

Holly has shared kennel space with setters most of her life, and they have all taken advantage of this gentle bear hug of a dog. Puppies whose names I can no longer remember thought she was a hairy medicine ball. One rogue got her pregnant; complications followed the abortion and I had Holly neutered. Another setter nailed Holly on the forehead. Even though she bit back and won the fight, it is she that carries a little hole between her eyes.

About four years ago we brought Holly into our house to live, and she has behaved like the good citizen she always was. I have never owned another dog that did not at least bark at the UPS drivers, but Holly offers a grin and a blockish head to pet. She approves of warm hands. A watchdog she is not.

Holly never messes in the house, does not beg, and knows her boundaries. On the other hand, over the years we have noticed an increasing sense of entitlement in direct proportion to the spread of whiteness across her muzzle. Holly refuses to take her pill unless my wife coats it first with peanut butter. She becomes instantly agitated whenever I pack for a trip, and when we do take her along she insists on riding in the front seat. If dogs could cry! "Insistence" takes the form of squinting eyes, a pink tongue in your face, the disappointed whap of an otterine tail along your leg.

The first time Holly smelled birds was the November day I chose her from the basement litter that was eight weeks old. She looked like one of those furry mitts used for washing cars. After sniffing my Bean boots, freshly worn in pheasant cover, she peed on them with excitement. These are the same boots with the chewed-away finger loops, a reminder that Holly once was a puppy. I still have them, somewhere, and probably always will.

Next year the first pheasant she flushed caused panic, then embarrassment, then a determination to put the boot to every ringneck on the continent. The following October she learned how to knock geese flat with nose-guard force. The setters were next. One of Holly's goals in life is to find a setter on point, then slamdunk the dog and take credit for the flush. I lecture her about this often, but she offers those Oriental eyes, grins, and trembles over her skillful revenge. This trait has grown so bad that I have had to attach a twelve-foot checkcord to Holly and tie her to aspens where she howls in misery until released for the retrieve.

Holly has gone everywhere with me, helping to collect game birds from deserts, mountains, plains, and woods. She has tasted all the native grouse and quails, pheasants from a dozen states, and doves, woodcock, partridge, and most species of waterfowl. In Nevada she blundered into a bobcat trap but escaped injury. Another time in Kansas she narrowly missed the strike of a prairie rattler. I have removed Missouri cockleburs, Oklahoma goatshead pickers, and Michigan porcupine quills from her feet, face, belly, and tail.

She has never complained.

Aging is a deceptive process, especially in a yellow Lab whose complexion masks a creeping gray face. I first noticed Holly's advancing age four years ago in the Colorado high country when she flagged behind and I, an out-of-shape flatlander, had to wait. In camp last fall she stole away early from our evening fire and found her bed in my tent. I know her hind legs ached from struggling to pull them over logs all day. I know because she licked my hands while I gently massaged her lower back and hips.

Later in Iowa, for the first time I can remember she did not bark when I unloaded a setter and left her in the truck. The dog ran wild and I kenneled him. I chose Holly and within five minutes she flushed a ringneck and delivered it with her patented soft retrieve. It was the kind of performance I have come to expect for a decade now but only learned to appreciate recently.

On trail you would never know Holly has a bowed back and drooping tail because she changes into a fluid blonde predator. She can make herself as slim as a nervous grouse about to flush. There is a youthful suppleness along with a determined economy to her movement. Holly hunts only where experience tells her birds might be. She knows exactly when I'll rein her in close, so why waste energy going out too far in the first place?

This fall Holly wants to migrate with woodcock throughout eastern North America. We have been sharing thoughts and plans on the subject for several months. As I write this, Holly lies in a yellow pool at my feet, muscles twitching from woodcock fluttering into her dreams.

I thumb through the calendar past too many pages to October.

Editor's Note: A couple of weeks after we received Tom Huggler's manuscript, he called to inform us that Holly had, indeed, passed away and that he had decided to put his travels for woodcock on hold. Huggler mentioned that Holly lies beneath an enormous beech, "wide as an elephant's ass," on his property. The beech commands a view of woodcock tangles and grouse uplands. The other night he flushed a ruffed grouse from its branches.

Charles Fergus is a freelance writer whose articles have appeared in many publications, including Shooting Sportsman, Game & Gun, Sporting Classics, Pennsylvania Game News, Science, Harrowsmith Country Life, *and* Audubon. *He is the author of four books. His first,* The Wingless Crow, *is a collection of essays on nature and country living. His historical novel,* Shadow Catcher, *deals with the 1913 Rodman Wanamaker Expedition of Citizenship to the North American Indian; a selection of the Book-of-the-Month Club, it is now out in paperback. Fergus has written two hunting books.* A Rough-Shooting Dog *chronicles the training and first hunting season of his English springer spaniel, Jenny;* Gun Dog Breeds *describes the more than thirty canine breeds used to hunt game birds in North America. Fergus lives with his wife, son, and spaniel in a stone house he built himself, on a mountain in central Pennsylvania, where grouse strut next to the woodpile and deer browse in the front yard.*

THE HEART
OF MY HUNTING

by Charles Fergus

It never seemed convenient. Hunting season was always just around the corner, and I didn't want her nursing puppies, or out of shape after having raised a litter, when the first day of grouse rolled around. I did not want a puppy for myself; I felt she should be my sole companion until she grew too old to put in a full day afield. So I kept putting it off, even though my hunting partners—after she'd made a particularly stirring flush or fetched a runner that surely would have fed the foxes—would scratch Jenny behind the ears, look at me, and ask, "When are you going to breed her?"

Jenny is an English springer spaniel. She is six years old, almost seven. Her coat is white, with patches of dark brown (technically, "liver") arrayed along her back and flanks, in what had looked to me, when she was a puppy, like the silhouette of a flushing grouse. Her tail is docked to about a foot in length, brown with an eye-catching white tip. Her eyes are golden-yellow. She has brown ears, a brown head, a white muzzle with a small brown mustache, and a symmetrical blaze on her forehead. Her shoulders reach to my knees. She is solid and muscular and, on the veterinarian's digital scale, weighs thirty-seven point six pounds.

Jenny is a rough-shooting dog. "Rough-shooting" is a British term that describes striking out across the land and taking whatever game the dog rousts out—precisely the sort of hunting Jenny and I practice here in central Pennsylvania.

To be sure, she is more than a hunting dog. She sounds the alarm when anyone drives down our lane. She can be counted on to join any sort of outing, be it a canoe trip, the one-hundred-yard walk to the mailbox, cross-country skiing (her first time out, she plunked down in the track to bite ice from between her pads, and suddenly we were both head-over-heels in the snow), my daily jog, picking blueberries (she strips them daintily from the stems with her front teeth and declines to drop them in the pail), hiking, bird watching, or simply puttering around in the yard. Jenny is a full-fledged member of our family, and confident in that status, but there is no question that she is my dog. Whenever the spirit moves her, which is often, she worms into my arms. She interposes herself between me and my four-year-old son when he and I are playing. Since she is not allowed on the furniture, she lays her head on my foot while I am sitting on the couch, reading. When I'm in my office writing, she curls up next to my chair.

Though she is not there now.

The house seems strangely empty. It has been like that all week. No friendly tail thumps when I lower a hand to pet her. No wagging and spinning at the door, as she lobbies to go outside. No gobs of white fur collecting in the corners, as my wife noted last weekend. However, I would bet that my wife, though she might not admit it, also misses Jenny.

On the bulletin board in my office is a list of five hunters who want a Jenny of their own. I would not have bred her just to satisfy these friends. But as Jenny matured—as she demonstrated the depth of her hunting instincts, her biddability and goodness of nature—I edged toward it. I did not make the

decision lightly. I weighed and pondered and analyzed (and probably anthropomorphized) before I acted.

I remember how long it took me to pick a breed of dog in the first place. Before I got Jenny, I hunted with acquaintances who ran pointing dogs: Brittanys, English setters, and pointers. I enjoyed watching those dogs work. They were terrific at pointing woodcock, less adept at handling pheasants and grouse.

When a dog went on point, all too often I would spy the pheasant or grouse, its head down and its body hunched, legging it off through the brush. Or the dog would "bump" the bird, flush it prematurely. My friends warned me not to shoot at birds so bungled: It would encourage the dogs to run riot. On the days when everything clicked and we managed to shoot a bird over a point, rare was the dog who would then go and fetch it. A dog might point a dead bird, helping us locate it, but that technique failed when a wounded bird took off running. All of this puzzled me greatly. I had always thought that one of the reasons for hunting with a dog—perhaps the main reason—was that it would fetch the game.

I considered what was being asked of a pointing dog: upon encountering scent, to freeze, fight down the instinct to rush in and grab the prey; and then, after the shot, to abandon this static stance, perhaps chase down a runner, pick the bird up gently but firmly, and bring it back. From what I had read, some paragons consistently managed those contradictory tasks. But I felt I lacked the skill and patience to train a pointing dog to that level.

I wanted a more basic sort of canine, one that simply flushed the game, hustled it into the air with a sudden, dramatic rush. More important, I wanted a dog I could depend on to retrieve the game I downed. My dog would hunt the gamut of upland birds: grouse, woodcock, pheasants, doves. Since I planned to expand my hunting to include ducks, I needed a dog that also would dive into the swamp and recover what I shot. According to the books I read, the English springer spaniel could do all of those tasks, with aplomb and good cheer. And I was charmed by the breed's looks: trim, efficient, rough-and-ready, a touch feral-looking with those raggedy high-set ears.

Spaniels At Play
by Arthur Wardle (English, 1864–1949)
Artwork courtesy of the William Secord Gallery, New York, NY 10021

It was a cool day in August, a day that spoke of autumn, when I went to pick up Jenny. The breeder let the mother and the puppies—three of the litter were left—out onto the lawn. I knelt and clapped my hands, and this double-handful of enthusiasm came tail wagging, ears flapping, as fast as her legs could carry her. I found it remarkable that a dog would so trust a strange human; but such is the nature of a puppy, open to love and to being loved. I have read about how early experiences imprint a creature and affect its behavior for the rest of its life. I became imprinted on Jenny at that moment, on that day in August of 1986.

I was thinking of that auspicious meeting—of the trust that Jenny had invested in me, and how it had grown and deepened—when I took her to the vet two weeks ago. I still had not decided whether to breed her, but I knew her time was limited. A six- or a seven-year-old bitch is far more likely to have problems whelping a litter than a three- or a four-year-old. If I was to breed Jenny at all, it would have to be during her next estrous.

What the veterinarian said added to my ambivalence. After examining her, he told me that Jenny had a constriction in her vagina. Some dogs, he said with a shrug, are just built that way. She might be able to accept a male, and she might not—in which case she could be bred through artificial insemination. That raised new questions in my mind. Once impregnated, would she be able to whelp? Probably, the vet said; and if need be, they could do a Caesarean section, a safe and routine procedure, some risk from the anesthesia, but usually without complications.

When Jenny and I got home that day, I grabbed my whistle and a pair of retrieving bucks. Down to the meadow we went, Jenny wagging her whole body and leaping for the dummies. This is old hat, but she loves it, loves to work, to do her job. I hupped her with a single blast on the whistle, threw a buck to one side, and heaved the second in the opposite direction. With a hand signal I sent her for the first buck; she raced to it and brought it back. I hupped her. *"Jenny!"* I said, releasing her for the second. She fetched it. I took the bucks, laid them down, and sat in the warm sun. Jenny sniffed the dummies, picked up one, and came and sat next to me.

When she was a puppy, she would carry all sorts of things in her mouth: sticks, pine cones, crumpled envelopes, corncobs filched from the compost heap, desiccated toads, songbirds that had broken their necks against the windows. Just holding something between her jaws seemed to make her feel secure. And how she loved to chase after the puppy buck—a small, kapok-filled boat bumper. She would pick it up with a flourish; her eyes knowing and her tail proud, she would dance it back to my hand.

One day—during her first October, when she was still too young to hunt—I shot a woodcock, carried it home, and hid it in the meadow. *"Jenny!"* I called, and waved her toward the bird. All gangly limbs and big paws, she romped along until she hit a tendril of scent—an essence she had never before encountered. She slammed to a halt, her body tense, her tail whipping from side to side. Guided by her nose, she sprang straight at the scent. Finding the source of that irresistible essence, she picked up the woodcock. I blew a few pips on the whistle. Fetching back, all the way she tried to stare at the strange feathery bundle between her jaws; it proved so enticing that she ran smack into my knee.

We spent hours in the meadow with whistle, buck, and gun. The guiding concept I drilled into her was *hup*. "Hup" is the traditional spaniel command for "sit." "Hup!" rockets out with authority to a dog on the edge of shotgun range, where "Sit!" may not be heard—or at least can be conveniently ignored. With that cornerstone firmly established, I could stop my spaniel on the trail of a running bird, so that I might get into position for a shot. Set her down when she got too near a road. Hide her at my side when ducks were flying. Halt her on a retrieve, then signal her to the bird.

I accustomed her to gunshots, to swimming, to riding in the canoe. Using planted birds (pigeons made dizzy and then hurled surreptitiously into the weeds), I tried to persuade her that the game always lay within twenty yards of the master's boots. Many were the Saturdays spent at a nearby shooting preserve run by a professional spaniel trainer; many were the pigeons, and finally the pheasants, that Jenny flushed and fetched. As we approached her second autumn, she had emerged as a spirited, hard-driving, raw, and promising young hunter.

One brisk October morning, we drove upstate in the dark, Jenny and I, and a friend and his young, equally inexperienced Labrador retriever. Dawn found us on the meandering headwaters of a stream, sneaking along, my friend and his dog on one bank, Jenny and I on the other. We crept past yellow-orange maples and deep green pines, through broad openings carpeted with tan grass and wine-red huckleberry. Frost lay heavily on the ground, and wisps of fog floated above the water.

Out ahead, we spotted a flock of wood ducks on a beaver pond. My friend and I crouched and began edging forward. Whispering fiercely, we held the dogs at heel. Soon our sneaking developed into a hunched-over race with the ducks' and the dogs' increasing awareness—until the flock finally took to the air with a chorus of keening cries. Our shotguns rang out. Two ducks fell.

My friend's duck was killed outright, but mine was only wounded. The dogs splashed around in a state of gleeful confusion. My duck, a wood duck hen, swam off into the brush. Coming in from the side, I spotted it only five yards ahead. Not wanting to obliterate it, I aimed a few inches in front of its bill. I pulled the trigger, the water spouted—and when it subsided, nothing was afloat. We searched for an hour. We combed the alders lining the banks. The dogs stuck their noses in every clump of brush, every patch of sedge. We looked upstream and down. Finally we gave up; we continued on with our hunt, but after a few hundred yards, we retraced our steps for one last look.

Jenny sniffed through a strip of grass we had searched maybe half a dozen times. The fur across her shoulders stood up. She pounced. The duck, peeping, went skidding down the bank in front of the spaniel and splashed into the run. Jenny crashed in after it but came up empty. I got her out and hupped her on the bank. After several minutes, my friend noticed two small bumps emerging from the water beneath the overhanging bank: the wood duck's eye and bill-tip. He shot. Jenny made the five-yard fetch.

I drove down the valley. The windshield wipers snick-ered. The creek, its surface dimpled with rain, ran brown and full on the south side of the road. Jenny sat on the floor, on the passenger's side, her front paws canted up onto the gearshift housing. She looked at me, then out the rear window. The trees along the road whisked by, the gray hills behind shifting more slowly. A crow flew across the road, and Jenny spotted it, her eyes widening, her ears raising, her tail sweeping the floor-boards.

I had decided. This was her chance, her first and last chance, to pass on that marvelous hunting sense, that loving merriness, that instinct coming down through countless gen-erations. That much she deserved.

The highway led past farms, houses, a lumberyard, a car dealership, a gravel pit. Beyond the creek, the land sloped upward toward Brush Mountain. Although it was late April, the mountain still looked like November, the trees gray-brown and bare. In the valley the lawns were greening, and weeping willows showed their tender yellow leaves. We left the main road and drove along a winding street. My friend's house, an old stone farmstead on three acres, is surrounded by newer homes. The settlement lies on the fringe of a small city that has been slowly crumbling for the last half-century, ever since its shops and yards—for repairing rail cars and building locomotives—shut down.

My friend let out his springer, and we went down by the creek. The male came after Jenny right away, sniffing at her tail, bumping her with his shoulders. She kept spinning around to face him. When he got too familiar, she growled him off.

The rain had slackened; my friend got a pigeon out of the bird pen, dizzied it, and threw it into the pond. Jenny swims like an otter (she has swum like that ever since she was a puppy—never that nervous forepaw-plunking that you see with some youngsters). With the male hupped on the bank, she paddled out, grabbed the pigeon, pirouetted in the water, and started back. Her white legs churned. Her eyes switched this way and that. She snorted water drops out of her nostrils. Her ears streamed back. Only the top of her head stayed dry.

We gave the male a retrieve. Then we let the dogs run. The male raced along close to Jenny, his side nudging hers. He licked Jenny's muzzle. He dropped to his belly, his rear end high and his tail wagging. She disdained to play with him. She came up to me, panting and wagging, a puzzled look on her face.

My friend's male, named Sky, is a young dog really coming into his own. Earlier this month, he placed third in a national pheasant competition held in Minnesota. Four years ago, my friend had gone to the Isle of Anglesey, off the coast of Wales, and bought the dog at the kennels of Talbot Radcliffe, the foremost springer spaniel breeder in the world. Sky's impeccable bloodline and his hunting prowess were not the only reasons I chose him: He is an experienced stud whom I hoped could effect the mating.

No luck that evening, though. Jenny would not stand for him; apparently she was not yet fully into estrous. It was dark when I said good-bye to her, there in the kennel by the creek. She barked plaintively as I crossed the lawn. I got in the truck and started for home. The traffic was light, and the rain had stopped.

The lights from a convenience store reflected off the black waters of the creek. Beyond loomed the mountain, dark and massive, probably with some good game cover tucked into its wooded folds. The combination of waters and woods got me thinking of another first from Jenny's first hunting season.

In the morning, I had shot two drake woodies on a beaver pond, with Jenny retrieving both; back home, I exchanged hip boots for Bean boots, and we went to the bottoms along the creek, where the land starts its gradual slope to the mountain. We tried a big patch of hawthorn and crab apples that always holds grouse. Halfway into the cover, she showed scent. The grouse powered up and cartwheeled at my shot. I went to my knees and spotted it crumpled on the ground beneath the crabs' arching stems. The grouse shot up its head. Its glittering eye took in the onrushing dog, and the bird picked itself up and raced off through the leaves. Jenny matched it swerve for swerve. It scuttled down over the bank toward the creek. So great was my confidence that I sat, unloaded the gun, and waited for Jenny to return. She did, with the grouse in her mouth, its eye angry and its crest upraised. My heart was pounding as I took it from her. This passing of game between dog and man is the heart of my hunting. I looked at my rough-shooting dog, and she at me.

· · · · ·

I swung the truck south at the light, gearing down for the hill. How far she had come since that first year! She had fetched many grouse—and would have fetched plenty more had I shot better. I would rather hunt grouse than any other game. One day last season, I wounded a big male and Jenny chased him down and brought him in. The grouse had his head up. He looked positively ferocious, outraged at having been apprehended. He did something decidedly ungrouselike: Turned his face toward Jenny's and pecked at her eye. I took the bird and dispatched him, then checked Jenny. She must have blinked before he got her, for her eye was unhurt. Then, on the last day of the season—just three months back, up a little hollow not two miles from where I was now driving—I flushed twenty-seven grouse in a bit under four hours, did not kill a one, and did not begrudge the birds a thing. They were wild as hawks (Did they know it was the last day?), and Jenny couldn't handle them. The last bird was an exception: She caught him hiding in a blowdown, and drove him up, straight at me. A big bird with a broad chestnut tail. I turned to take him going away. He juked behind a bushy hemlock, and I never saw him again.

I stopped at another traffic light. The light changed, and I went east. Down the valley I drove. A good brushy valley where lights are few. I passed a shuttered-up country store, an auto body shop, an old barn with a hole battered in its brick side. Across the railroad tracks from the barn, on the other side of the stream, lies the covert I call Pufferbelly.

I named the covert that day, back in Jenny's first year, when an antique steam engine came chugging incongruously down the line. A gray day, with a chill wind to hurry the clouds. Quick showers of rain pattered against the fallen yellow leaves. The smoke from the locomotive hung like a banner above the tracks, then began shredding. We started from the east, into the wind. Immediately Jenny set to work with an almost frantic busyness to her quartering. Her lithe white form coursed through the brush like a predatory fish hunting in the shallows. The clouds parted for a moment, light slanting in through the break, lending a coppery tone to the aspens' water-beaded bark. Chalk on the ground, and holes made by bills probing for worms. Things can develop quickly—and often unpredictably—when you follow a flushing dog. The scent practically yanked her around. The woodcock came up like a gusted leaf. Wings twittering, following its mud-flecked bill, it swerved a course through the close-set trunks. My shot downed it on the far side of the creek. Jenny swam across, ferreted the bird out of the dense willows, and paddled back, her first woodcock dangling loose-headed and long-beaked from her jaws.

· · · · ·

When I got back home, I looked at Jenny's empty kennel box. I sat down to read for a while, and no spaniel came to lay her head on my foot. I put the book down.

Was I tempting fate? I still did not think I wanted a pup for myself. I certainly wasn't breeding her for the money any puppies would bring. A friend once remarked that he was breeding his purebred dogs to put his kids through college. Put the vet's kids through college, is more like it.

So why press the issue? The next bitch I get, I'll have her spayed right off so I won't have to make these decisions. Had I done right by Jenny? Puppies were a tremendous drain on a dog, especially an older one. There was probably still time to call it off, the dogs were kenneled together but it didn't look like Sky would make any progress tonight.

But I didn't call. Pass it on, girl, I thought. If you can. That prebreeding exam—finding the constriction in her vagina—still bothered me. Artificial insemination? No. If she couldn't breed on her own, we'd forget it.

I sat in the quiet house, considering how much it meant to me, having Jenny. I remembered what was probably the brightest day of our first year's hunting. It was so cold that morning that my hands were alternately numb and then wracked with pain. Jenny had dipped her belly in the creek, and icicles tinkled when she wagged.

The decoys bobbed in the olive-drab water. A mallard quacked from somewhere downstream. Suddenly, there they were! Black ducks! Four pairs of wings came pumping, cupping, fluttering down—but the ducks flared up and began to flee. I managed to shove the safety off. I swung on the first duck in line, yanked the trigger, missed, shot again, apparently missed—and heard a splash. A duck, from farther back in line, floated upside down in the creek. "Jenny!"—and out she went into the frigid flow. Swimming hard, she gathered him in and was swept downstream by the current. She fought her way over to the bank. I stumbled through the brush and mud to meet her.

That afternoon, on a snowy hillside strewn with logging slash, she flushed and fetched a brace of grouse. Our hunt finished, we trudged home along the logging path as slivers of pink and yellow glowed in the gray western sky. I walked loose-limbed and weary, basking in the sense that I understood, really understood, what it meant to collaborate with a dog. To expand my instincts in partnership with a creature whose talents far surpassed mine. To let her joyousness, her simplicity, rub off on me. To shed mind and intellect for a time, to soak up the hunt, to simply be myself. I called her to me. As she danced around, her eyes on the cover, still wanting to get in there and hunt, I aimed caresses at her head. I ran my hand down her back and crooked it where her muscular hind leg joined her belly. I pulled her against my own leg, held her there for a moment, and told her what a good dog she was. With a perfunctory tail wag she broke free, and, glancing over her shoulder, tried to lure me back into the slash. I smiled and patted my palm against my thigh; reluctantly, she came back to heel. She had no need to stop and ponder, no need to hoard memories. For her, there was only the sweet now.

· · · · ·

Another evening, in the truck again; the moon was setting in the west behind coal-sack clouds as I headed for home. Tonight it was done—though she will stay with the male for a while yet.

She was ready. She was flagging her tail, wanting it to happen despite the discomfort causing her to yelp and pull away. I ended up holding Jenny, talking quietly to her, and there was blood and pain, and then calm, and, for the humans at least, elation. Who knows what the dogs thought and felt?

There will be more blood and pain nine weeks hence. I hope someday to write a postscript about healthy young spaniels on their way to good homes, to lives that are rich with love of master and land and game and the consuming, fulfilling passion of the hunt. I hope to write a postscript about an old rough-shooting dog back home in the fields and marshes, the beaver dams, the thornapple patches, the alder tangles, having passed on her brief, glowing spark.

Thomas McIntyre is the long-time Hunting Editor of Sports Afield *magazine where he writes the "Hunting" and "A Hunter's View" columns. His hunting and fishing travels have carried him to five continents, from the High Arctic to Australia, Africa, and New Zealand, and from the Czech Republic to Hawaii. His essays and short stories have appeared in over a dozen anthologies, and he is the author, as well, of three works of non-fiction, the most recent being* Dreaming the Lion: Reflections on Hunting, Fishing, and a Search for the Wild *published in the fall of 1993 by Countrysport Press. Tom, his wife Elaine, their young son Bryan Ruark, and their two dogs, Bubba and Beckett, divide their time between southern California and northern Wyoming.*

BLANCA

by Thomas McIntyre

"Where's that dog?"

I stood in the shaft of cool February sunlight falling through the doorway, my eyes adjusting to the darkness within the adobe house. Pete sat on the three-legged sofa, a brick propping up the broken corner and a Navajo blanket concealing the holes in the upholstery. On the wall behind him hung a cane fly rod and a wicker creel, beneath it an A. H. Fox 16-gauge, displayed like heraldic devices. He laid the Badminton Library book on coursing he was reading beside him on the sofa, opened, on top of the pile of other old books, and stood. His boots kicked up small billows of dust as he crossed the carpet. I stepped into the overheated house, and Pete and I exchanged *abrazos* and backslaps. Sally came out of the kitchen dressed in a flannel shirt and faded jeans, and when I leaned down to kiss her I smelled in her hair the smoke of the cigarettes she'd been sneaking outside, the cancer that would kill her in less than a year already shadowing through her lungs.

"Let's see her," I said.

They led me to a doorway off the living room. The door had been removed from its hinges and set crosswise inside on the floor across the bottom of the door frame, making a two-and-a-half-foot-high barrier. The room had been emptied of furniture and through the single curtainless window I could see in the distance bare cottonwoods along a wash and a pickup moving down the highway toward El Paso. The floor of the room was covered with flattened cardboard boxes, covered with newspapers, rags, torn sheets, and feces, and wet with urine. A large pan of water and one of dry food sat in the far right corner of the room.

Jesse-Bell stood with her front paws on the edge of the door, barking with each breath as she had been since before I'd walked into the house. Pete moved forward, taking her head in his hands and shaking her playfully. "Hush, now, Jess honey," he insisted, and the liver-and-white springer began to grin at him, wriggling the four-inch stump of her tail.

Pete stepped over the door and into the room, and I followed, the bitch backing away from me and growling softly, showing me her front teeth. The six pups, liver-and-white and black-and-white, clustered in the far left quarter of the room, exhibiting a sort of Brownian motion as they fought and rolled and yipped and played. Pete waded into them and lifted a black-and-white one by its fat eight-week-old belly.

"Here you are," he said, handing the pup to me. Its tail was docked, and I lay it on its back in the crook of my arm and saw it was a female. At once she began to squirm and to yelp sharply.

"Pick of the litter," Pete said, smiling, slipping his hands into the front slash pockets of his Wranglers so he could not readily reach out again to accept the pup back from me. She was squirming too hard now to hold, so I squatted and placed her on the floor.

"Pick of the litter," I repeated.

"Set her aside especially," Pete replied.

I watched her as she began worrying the sheet. "How much you asking?"

For you—for Big Ed? Three hundred."

The pup had hunkered down to pee now. She had a wide saddle of white on her back. While Pete and I were in the nursery, Sally had gone to the kitchen and come back with two tall plastic picnic glasses half filled with ice and sour mash.

Grinning, she handed the drinks over to us, and we each took a pull from them.

"She'll make him a good dog," Pete said, rocking gently on his heels, his left hand in his pocket and his drink held against his chest.

"What are you going to call her?" Sally asked, as if the deal were done. I looked at Sally's smiling face, and then Pete's, then at the pup's saddle of white. She was a dog meant to make all the difference in the world.

"Blanca," I said, raising my glass to Pete.

· · · · ·

In the driveway I sat with my hands on the wheel, the engine switched off and the heat ticking out of it. Beside my car was parked the Roadmaster on which, over the years, Big Ed had replaced every moving part with his own hands. As I sat I was letting the highway replay itself inside my head, first the high plateau in the dark, the green spark of a shooting star arcking across the sky, then the canyon at sunrise, the big hill down to the saguaros, and the long desert run through the day to the pass and the basin filled with fouled air at sunset. Eating while I drove, I'd stopped only for gas and every few hours at a rest area to let Blanca out of her carrier to walk around on the lead, starting to work with her on heeling while white-haired snow-birds stared at us over their tuna-fish sandwiches, wanting to make sure I wasn't going to let her shit next to their recreational vehicles. I'd traveled so quickly because I hadn't wanted to waste a minute getting her back.

Now Blanca was asleep in the carrier in the back seat of the Land Cruiser. I looked into the windows of the house, looking for any lights within. The house appeared abandoned, but I could see a faint blue glow coming from the living room. I sat for a minute more, then got out of the car.

I opened the rear door of the car and unlatched the gate on the carrier, lifting the sleeping pup out, tucking her under my left arm. Pulling open the screen door, I found the front door of the house unlocked and I entered, walking through to the living room. Dan Rather was just wishing everyone goodnight. On top of the set stood a dusty pair of mounted chukar.

Big Ed sat in his green leather armchair, looking shrunken in his clothes. For several seconds he did not notice me standing beside him. Then he lifted his head and stared at me through the tops of his bifocals, his eyes large and wet behind the lenses.

"I've got something for you," I said, offering the pup.

Big Ed blinked, recognition ebbing into his expression. His eyes moved from my face to the pup in my hands.

"Her name's 'Blanca," I said.

Big Ed now saw the little dog I was holding toward him, and for a moment he didn't seem to know what to do. Then he reached out his large hands for her, drawing her into his lap. He petted her gently and Blanca nestled back into her sleep.

I went into the kitchen and turned on the lights. In the wash rack by the sink were a plate, a knife, and a fork. I opened the refrigerator. Inside stood a carton of milk, a carton with two eggs left in it, half a stick of butter on a dish, a loaf of bread, a package of boiled ham, a squeeze-bottle of yellow mustard. I went outside and got the carrier, the lead, and the bag of puppy food I bought before leaving Pete and Sally's and brought them into the kitchen.

Walking back into the living room, I found that Big Ed had switched on the lamp beside his chair and was studying the sleeping Blanca as he softly stroked her, smiling to himself. On the stand was the framed twenty-five-year-old photograph of Big Ed and Joan and me, laid flat. On the TV set, beside the chukar, stood another framed photo of Big Ed, his hair still black in those days, showing him kneeling beside his old springer Bubba, Ed holding his Model 12, half-a-dozen Gambel's quail arranged on the rocky ground in front of him and the dog.

"Let me buy you supper," I said. Big Ed, still smiling and petting the pup, shook his head. "I've eaten."

"All right," I said. I reached into my shirt pocket and pulled out the folded sheet of yellow legal paper Pete had written out for me and lay it on the lamp stand, covering our photograph.

"Here are her feeding instructions," I said. "She's got enough food for a week, and I'll buy some more when she needs it. I'll take care of her papers for you, and I'll take her to the vet when her shots are due."

I hesitated, wondering if he'd heard me.

"They say she'll make a good dog," I said. "I'll help you work with her, if you want."

Big Ed nodded slowly, still smiling down at the curled up puppy.

"Don't worry," he said. "I can take care of her." He looked up at me. "We'll do just fine."

I wanted to reach out and put my hand on his shoulder, but instead I just nodded and turned to go.

When I reached the front door, I heard Big Ed's voice behind me in the living room. "Thank you," he said.

· · · · ·

The phone rang three times before I picked up the receiver.

"Hello," I said.

There was silence on the other end, but a silence tenanted by someone. I waited, not wanting to say hello again, wanting to let him have the time to find the words that seemed to be coming harder and harder every day.

"I'm having trouble with her," Big Ed finally said. "Blanca. I don't think I can handle her anymore."

"What kind of trouble?"

Big Ed did not answer. After more seconds of silence he said, "I think you'd better take her."

"I'll be over," I said, holding onto the receiver until, at last, Big Ed put down his.

When I crossed the bridge, the concrete bed of the river was dry, the steeply sloped banks tagged with spray-painted insignia. The spreading grounds still held rainwater, percolating down to the water table to be pumped out again; but all the sprigs that had swum on that water through the winter, as incongruous in the city as orchids on a fire hydrant, were gone now, only a few coots remaining. Just past the river I turned down a cul-de-sac and parked once more in Big Ed's driveway.

In the kitchen Big Ed was bracing himself up with one hand on the edge of the sink as he drank a glass of water from the tap. He looked at me over the rim of the glass as he finished, then turned and carefully rinsed the glass, placing it in the empty wash rack. He turned nervously back to me, as if he were preparing to flinch. A six-month-old Blanca ran barking into the kitchen and looked at us both, then ran off again.

"I just don't know how to handle her anymore," Big Ed said.

"That's all right," I said. "We've talked about this."

"I just don't know," he said.

I walked into the living room and saw where Blanca had just peed on the carpet, other places that Big Ed had not cleaned up visible as well. One of the arms on the green chair had been chewed through, the stuffing showing. Blanca ran excitedly around the room, then turned and crouched at me to bark, before racing off again.

I managed to haze her into one of the corners of the room and scooped her up, struggling in my arms, strong as a piglet. I carried her back to the kitchen and pushed her into her carrier.

Big Ed still stood by the sink, looking neither at the carrier nor me, but out the window at his narrow backyard where a crow hopped on the lawn.

"It's time to take her to the trainer anyway," I said, Big Ed making no acknowledgement of my words. I picked up the dog box and carried it outside to the back seat of the Land Cruiser, Blanca barking continuously inside.

As I turned to go back into the house, Big Ed was standing behind the screen door, barring my entry.

"A few months with the trainer," I said to him through the screen, "and she'll be fine."

Big Ed didn't say anything, just stared at the Land Cruiser.

"A few months," I said, "and she'll be ready for us to take her hunting."

"I just don't know what to do with her," Big Ed said. Then he stepped back from the screen and closed the front door.

· · · · ·

The Mexican in the blue ball cap was hosing out one of the dog runs when I drove in and parked in front of the kennel's office. Inside, Corrigan sat behind his desk, fat and hung over, talking on the phone. He waved me to the chair across the desk from him.

"...the entire science of animal training's changed tremendously in the past twenty years since we've learned more about animal behavior," he was saying to a potential client. "Well, sure, you can find somebody who says he'll train your dog for less, but what kind of a dog do you get back? That's the question...No, you go ahead and think it over...Anytime. Glad to help." Replacing the receiver, he folded his arms and leaned forward on his desk, looking at the phone. "Assholes," he said. He looked at me, the veins webbed red across his cheeks. "Like I always say, The problem is never the dog, it's the fucking owner." Pushing himself to his feet, he walked around the desk and toward the front door. "Come on," he said as I stood, "let's see what that little bitch of yours can do."

We drove off the hill and out onto the flood plain. Corrigan opened the door on one of the compartments of the dog carrier that took up the back of his pickup and lifted Blanca out. He clipped a long white rope to her collar and handed the end to me. I could see how in only a few months she had changed from puppy to a dog. Corrigan opened another compartment and took out a pigeon, cupping its body in his hand, its head held between two of his fingers. Then, holding the pigeon next to his body, he got his over-and-under out from behind the seat of his pickup, breaking it open with one hand and laying it over the crook of his arm that held the pigeon. He slipped in a couple of No. 7 1/2 loads and then took the rope end from me.

"We talked about making this dog into a slip retriever, didn't we?" he asked. "I just wanted to make sure."

As he walked out across the willow stubble I hung back. Blanca ranged off a few yards to his right and just slightly ahead of him, staying within the length of the rope. About fifty yards out, Corrigan dropped the rope and lifted the over-and-under off his arm, then threw the pigeon into the air. As the bird fluttered for a moment to get its bearing, Corrigan closed his shotgun and when the pigeon started to fly away, he dropped it thirty yards from him with his bottom barrel. Blanca had been watching this procedure curiously, and at the sound of the shot she stiffened, then turned and ran off to the right, making a large circle back to the pickup, crawling beneath it as Corrigan cursed.

The noon sunlight cast the shadow of Corrigan's brows over the red veins of his cheeks as he broke open his gun and stomped back toward the pickup, shouting, "You no-good piece of shit," as he came. I walked back to the pickup first and squatted down. Blanca stared out at me from underneath it. I snapped my fingers at her a few times and reluctantly she came out. I had her in my arms when Corrigan got to us.

"Give me that goddamn dog," he said, throwing his shotgun onto the seat of the pickup through the open door.

"No," I said.

"That dog wasn't much," he shouted, his red hands kneading the air in front of him, "but she was coming on. What screwed her up was you being here.

"It's you talking baby-talk to these damn dogs, then expecting me to train them, to make something real out of them. You don't have any idea what a real dog is supposed to be. You could take a stick and beat a pup every day and still make it a real dog. But all you want to do is talk baby-talk to these goddamn dogs, and all you end up with is a piece of shit like this."

He was starting to run out of steam as I put Blanca back into her compartment in the dog carrier and closed the door. His hands had dropped to his sides, heavy and limp, when I turned back to him.

"Let's go back to your office now and I'll settle my account with you."

"Useless piece of shit," he said, but by now he was saying it to himself.

· · · · ·

Blanca was barking when I got home from downtown. I took the Model 12 with the tag on the trigger guard and the manila envelope out of the Land Cruiser and carried them into the garage, laying them on the work table. I walked into the backyard and Blanca ran up to me, rolling onto her back at my feet as I reached down to pet her. I changed the water in her bowl and gave her two cups of dry food for her dinner.

In the garage I opened the manila envelope and removed the two items in it. One was the gold wedding band, the other the pair of bifocals marked with dried flecks of blood. I put the wedding band into my shirt pocket and dropped the glasses into the trash barrel beside the work table. No one had wanted the Roadmaster, so I sold it to a wrecking yard. I clamped the Model 12 into the vice on the table and got down the hacksaw.

As I sawed I could hear Blanca barking in the backyard, and in my mind I could see her standing rigid, the stump of her tail up, barking at nothing I could ever see. It was then I realized that, like Big Ed, I didn't know what to do with her any more than he had. She was as useless to me as she had been to him.

· · · · ·

It was late one night when Pete called. Sally had been dead for over two years. Pete was drunk.

"How's that dog of yours?" he shouted.

I told him that she was fine.

"Showed her many birds?"

No, not many birds at all, I said.

"You got to show her more birds," Pete insisted.

Yes, I agreed with him.

"But you have to be careful," Pete said. "You have to be careful she doesn't run away. If you're not, she'll be gone before you know it. And might never get her back."

· · · · ·

I wore my own wedding band now, and Blanca never did make a dog. She was nine and Owen was two. At night, after his bath, Owen would come out and stand beside me as I sat in my armchair, reading the paper. I would pretend for a moment not to notice him, and he would pretend that he did not notice me, intently watching his fingers as they played with one another. Then I would fold the paper and put it down and I would stare at Owen. In a little while, without really looking up, he would lift his arms to me and I would pull him up to me, hugging him to my chest and smelling the scent of his clean hair, of spices like cloves and nutmeg, feeling the coolness of his cheek against mine, and hearing the beginnings of his giggles. And wishing that I knew a way in this world for Big Ed to have done the same, if only once.

I never did learn what to do with Blanca. As she'd gotten older she'd just seemed to get crazier and more useless. I had to watch Owen when he was in the yard with her, because I had seen her snap at him more than once if he got too close. But I still could not find a reason to take that stick to her or to have her put down. There was still too much of unfinished business about her, too much of a gesture made that had gone somehow unseen. Or that had been the wrong gesture to begin with.

One day, when we were packing our household belongings into moving crates, Celeste came in and asked me if I'd looked at Blanca lately.

She lay on the carpet in her house, seeming very subdued, nearly depressed, and I noticed that she looked bloated, bigger than I had ever seen her. Not fat, but swollen. Then I saw the large tumor on one of her teats.

At the office, the veterinarian asked me to lift her onto the stainless-steel examination table, because he had long ago flagged her file jacket with a red sticker that read, "Bites." While I held her head, he felt her other nipples and said that the tumors had already spread to them. Then he did not speak for a few moments, before saying that there really was not much that could be done. I asked him if I could stay there with her, and he said, Of course.

I signed the release slip authorizing the euthanasia, then while I held her and stroked her softly, the vet felt on her leg for the vein. Strangely, Blanca didn't try to struggle at all, staying utterly quiet the entire time. The vet warned me that she might go into convulsions as the drug took effect, but she would feel no pain. Then he slipped the needle of the large syringe filled with the pink drug into her vein, drawing back a small plume of blood into the barrel, then slowly depressed the plunger.

Blanca didn't struggle or convulse at all, just held my eye in hers. As I felt her growing limp in my arms, I began to cry for the first time since I was a child—I hadn't even been able to cry for Big Ed, but now there were tears for such a sorry dog as this. I kept saying to her, "That's a good girl. That's a good girl." And at that moment, as perhaps at no other time in her life, she was a good girl. As her heart was stopping, it was as if she wanted to show me her true heart after all.

I walked out of the office into the hazy sun of late afternoon, wrapping Blanca's lead and collar around my hand, wondering what "useless" really means. Is any dog completely useless, does any sign of love truly go unseen?

Gary Marek lives in the Boardman River valley south of Traverse City, Michigan, a few miles from the stretch of river where Len Halliday created the Adams dry fly. The Boardman is still a good home to the Adams, pockets of grouse, and woodcock with a taste for tag alder. Marek resides with his wife, Arta, and a teenage daughter, Brooklynne, in a questionable house that nevertheless sits within a few hundred feet of swamp-edge woodcock and grouse. He has written for a variety of publications, including Fly Rod & Reel, Gray's Sporting Journal, and Audubon. *He continues to believe that fishing and bird hunting are his best means of discovering essential truths.*

IN PRAISE OF PORCUPINES AND OTHER MEN'S DOGS

by Gary Marek

I felt the needle seek deeper territory. "So, is yours steady to wing and shot?" the orthopedic surgeon asked with genuine interest. I was off guard in every way. I hadn't even thought about such an irrelevant and rarified subject in years. Hell, *I'm* not steady to wing and shot, I reminded myself. I managed a meditative groan and felt some of the prepatory swab liquid run from my shoulder down the back of my arm. It began to drip off the point of my elbow.

"Yeah, hang in there now. Here—let me clean that up a bit." I had just noticed that the rivulet felt a bit heavy and slow. "Sometimes there's a little blood with one of these, but it won't be too much longer now," he added.

Finally, my head cleared itself away from the area where pain and cortisone simultaneously rushed deep into my entire shoulder. My favorite shoulder, where right-side movements of great physical importance were controlled and carried out, like fly casting and handling a 20-gauge shotgun.

"She's steady to wing" (a lie) "but not to shot," I said as casually as I could. It was my second visit to this young surgeon and what we shared in common besides an interest in the storms of pain brewing within my right shoulder and upper arm was ownership of German shorthaired pointers. Mine was nine years old, an aging if not old hunter. His was a two-year-old adolescent, a carefully trained but "unfinished" sporting dog with lots of potential. I had recently come to see myself as a bird dog realist; the surgeon was still an optimist pursuing cherished images and the creation of a canine laser with all of its sophisticated energies precisely aligned. A focused and empowered individual, as people of the nineties like to say.

The needle was out, the wound swabbed and bandaged, and I felt anything but empowered. "Actually, now I just go hunting when I can. I let her run and hope for the best," I added. This could get touchy. I wasn't in the mood for debate, swagger, or poignant testimonials, and to avoid the treachery of different field theologies I decided to play commoner to his erudite skills and membership in elite professional societies. And it was true that I still hadn't returned his two expensive dog-training videos. The starring dogs were automatons of perfection.

Sometimes I'm amazed that I even have a bird dog, I went on to say. We finished our cortisone encounter with a second and almost evil shot into the top of the right elbow. My shooting hand and forearm would be lubed in no time. I drove home left-handed to my shorthair and gun-shy vizsla and, perhaps because blood was still in the air, spent the rest of the afternoon reflecting about the mysterious personae of hunting dogs and the humans they tolerate or love or dominate.

· · · · ·

I did not understand the long vowels and mournful language of the new beagle next door. While I loved the pounding rhythms of Eddie Cochran and Buddy Holly by day, the

midnight wailing of this, this *hound dog*, was annoying even to an essentially brainless kid whose greatest concern in 1958 involved the quantity of frogs he was going to spear in Indian Mill Creek near Farmer Pete's slaughterhouse. During that long and very hot summer, I was introduced to blood sport (I now prefer the term food gathering) and the sporting breeds.

My best friend lived a few blocks away and while hanging around my house one night after we'd picked some nightcrawlers he took note of our neighbor's howling beagle. "We've got one near us, too. They're *hunting dogs*, you know. They're different." My friend is a psychologist now and still believes they're different. He has acquired a new golden retriever that (I refuse to invoke the personal pronoun who) receives occasional foot massages from his wife to reduce the energy field the dog carries with it every waking moment. If the golden's behavior doesn't come around I expect the burgeoning dog chiropractic movement might reach my friend's house someday as well.

I lost track of hunting dogs for nearly two decades after the beagle and frog summer but developed a sideways-glance interest again when I turned from a birdwatching anti-hunter (I could snap my Bushnells on target as fast as anyone in the woods) into a tag-a-long hunting agnostic. I even thought it might be interesting to acquire a bird dog someday so I could walk along and take pictures while friends tried to shoot birds. I had heard watching a good dog at work in the woods was a little like fly fishing—aesthetically pleasing.

Springer spaniels appealed to me and I finally decided to surprise my wife with a ten-week-old male as an early anniversary present. As she petted and cooed at him I felt his obvious intelligence measure us through slightly enigmatic eyes. Not many weeks later and well before he reached his physique of steel, he vaulted into the air and sank his small teeth into my wife's midriff. Apparently, she was not supposed to enter the room at that moment. I was thankful that he was unable to spring a bit higher.

"The best thing you can do is hunt him. Repetition and the smell of birds. Get him out there as often as you can," an avid bird hunting friend from Leelanau County advised. The reactions to his behavior problems were consistent: bird dogs are high-spirited creatures that need to hunt. "But remember—he's a flusher so you aren't going to see any points. Then again, that's not so terrible. Springers work close and get all wiggly when they're onto a bird. Just take him to birds and he'll end up tired and happy."

After many years of quiet opposition to hunting, I still wasn't ready to begin wielding a shotgun, but I did have another close friend who grew up with a springer ("Heidi, the greatest mouser in the history of the world!" he would brag) and wanted to convert me to the brotherhood of the long gun. He would be glad to give my dog some work.

· · · · ·

"Gary, you don't need to do that, honest!" My friend seemed a little exasperated. I was only trying to be safety conscious by instantly dropping to my knees when a bird flushed within range. It was the inverse of the soldier's "incoming!" When there were outgoing flights, I hit the dirt. In future outings I began to do much better and decided my partner wasn't going to cooly swing on a woodcock and accidently ventilate me. Unfortunately, after a promising outing or two my young springer began to act erratically and even stopped working periodically to sulk. I am certain my air-raid behavior had nothing to do with it. Then one day in Ghidra's Cover (named after a huge woodcock reminiscent of those Japanese film monsters) he decided to stage a real sit-down strike. I quickly tired of dragging a 60-pound dog through thick aspen and carried him most of the way back to my cabin. He was not tired. His eyes were both distant and demonic.

I soon retired as a bird-hunting sidekick and our bird dog continued to alternate between affection so touching that he was "almost like another person" as all dog owners say sooner or later, and a rabid Cerberus.

On the eve of my wife's thirty-second birthday and in the fifth month of her pregnancy with our only child, he did us a great favor: he drew real blood. This time he attacked my wife with full Jekyll-and-Hyde fury. Persona lifted, anima revealed. Serious injury was averted only through luck and a frantically slammed bedroom door. In the morning we drove him into town in the front seat of our pickup while he licked our faces and remained oblivious to the psychotic episode of the evening before.

At the vet's I put his favorite blanket with him, stroked his soft feathers, and whispered I was sorry. Two hours later he was dead by lethal injection. I am certain that if he had lived he would have tried to kill our baby daughter. Years later I was fortunate enough to learn from a magazine article and eventually other sources that he undoubtedly suffered from what some dog experts call Springer Rage. It was a relief but an anticlimax.

My bird dog ownership days were over.

· · · · ·

And my hunting days suddenly began. Heidi's owner sold me his old Italian side-by-side 20-gauge and took me back into the woods, this time without the camera. That same autumn another good trout fishing friend invited me to join him and his dog Meg, a somewhat cerebral but still pleasant vizsla. Among a small circle of friends and relatives, Meg's reputation for understanding the full importance of bird hunting inspired reverential tones.

This was in the Dark Ages Before Electronic Collars and Training Videos. However, according to Meg's owner, Ted, she was as enthusiastic as a "two-peckered billygoat" in the presence of birds and had developed a precise lifestyle. That is, she rested during winter and spring, went on commando vegetable raids and grasshopper pointing sorties in the family garden during summer, and then centered herself on bird business as autumn arrived. Apparently it had taken some mistakes and a few years of mutual alignment, but she and Ted had made it official: they were man and bird dog.

The first precept that these two friends (I quickly perceived that Meg wasn't aloof but simply a focused professional) destroyed for me was the myth that hunting grouse and woodcock was difficult or complicated. Sure, learning how to shoot properly and especially hitting canon-fired grouse or those diurnal bats with long bills that whistle up from underfoot is always difficult, but the rest was quite simple. We followed Meg until she shifted into a slow-motion creep or froze on point. Ted moved up to flush the bird, or if one of us happened to be closer we followed his quick, traffic-cop commands and "walked up" the bird ourselves. If one of us hit the bird, the red dog would find it and take it to Ted. He is a superior shot with gunslinger quickness, which means that the bird more often than not belongs in his vest. But if it were downed by a partner, the bird was quickly removed from Meg's grinning chops and handed over. That was that. Simple. Almost a system, as the technocrats would say.

Never was the ease of bird hunting more clear to me than during my second season of hunting. I had rationalized the shame and depressive effects of going zero for fifty during a preseason warm-up skeet shoot with Ted and two other close friends at an abandoned prison camp softball field. I could still hear the sympathetic voices assuring me that "you nicked that one for sure I think," but a year had passed, I had logged a fair amount of hours in the woods alone, and I'd killed a few birds. I also sensed acceptance; my three bird hunting friends were now of the opinion that I wasn't going to trim off an ear or mangle a shoulder with careless excitement if a bird happened to fly between us. And perhaps just as important, Ted deduced that I wasn't going to shoot Meg. Therefore, he wouldn't have to worry about shooting me and damaging our friendship.

The light of an early October dawn charged me with energy. Hoarfrost surrounded my cabin. With the overripe peach smell of freshly split red oak in my hands, I rekindled the fire and slipped into my almost furry nylon-faced hunting pants. Hunting without dogs tears at skin and frays clothing with an unrefined kind of violence. I would need a new pair, maybe one with Cordura armor, next year. October bird mornings are crisp but they are also uncomplicated and full of assurance. With just a little effort, the cold air becomes warm, the fall woods become artistic blends, and the day is ours.

Only minutes later Meg reached my cabin door well before Ted and his brother Bill. Once again she was convinced this would be the best day of her life.

A short drive put us in the woods listening to the high jingling of a working dog's bell. Meg's breath appeared and

disappeared like puffs of sentinel smoke. Wet with the soften-
ing frost dripping from still green ferns, she gleamed with an
aura of antiquity like a burnished cello.

As sudden as a released breath, the sound of a grouse
halted us. But it vanished. Then another, also out of range and
made only of faint reverberations deflected by motionless shafts
of maple and aspen.

"She's creeping! Could be a covey!" Ted strained to
mute his voice. Pressing a shutter and pulling a trigger do not
create equal amounts of passion and concentration. I was more
conscious than I had been in a very long time. "She's on. Over
here Bill—Gary go ahead! Walk up to Meg. Meggy you stay!" But
nothing happened as I thoroughly moved around the frozen
dog. I felt as if I could hear a spider take a step from one leaf to
another. Suddenly she broke twenty feet toward Ted and his
brother Bill, then stopped on point again. Ted thought a
running grouse might be in front of us, but after some wandering around, he explained for my benefit that she probably was
pointing where the birds had been walking moments earlier.
We were beginning one of those impromptu breaks during
which the hunters try to calm down and reconcile a nearly ideal
and lost opportunity (*If only I'd walked around that windfall, I
would've had a clear...*).

I listened to droplets of water fall from trees and strike
the lemon and vermillion forest floor as if it were fabric. Air now
bright with morning sun moved slightly through the tall grasses
of the large field behind my cabin. The open land hadn't been
disturbed by anything but deer hooves for over sixty years. Ted
tried to call Meg back to us and Bill laughed at her staunch
devotion to an evaporating scent. I tried to imagine the field
defined by the giant white pines of a century ago, but hunting is
a vital counterpoint to thinking and I couldn't organize thought
and emotion. I decided that on this day I was a part of the forest
and the field in the same way colossal trees once had been.

Ted swung and fired so quickly that for a heartbeat, the
entire woods filled with movement. The roar of grouse and
shotgun converged and almost as quickly were joined by a red
dog weaving toward us with a large grouse. Ted giggled through
glee and crooned *good girl* repeatedly. Apparently sane dogs

enjoy baby talk. This is pretty nice, I was thinking. Real bird dogs even find and send you birds out of trees. I wondered if woodcock ever spent much time in trees but didn't want to interrupt the effusive dog praise with a question. Bill repeated *unbelievable* enough to bore the dog and drive her into a slink toward cover. I wore out *awesome* and began to look at hemlocks with new perspective. Like all great dogs she could smell a thought if it involved the birds of passion.

The tree grouse set off a bird pointing seminar that ended with the three of us washed with the earthen aroma of spent shells, a good number of birds against the small of our backs, and a dog that had gone from a high-stepping, allegro pace through the ferns and trees to a posture that seemed to say, I'll hunt until I die but I wouldn't turn up my snout at an intermission right now.

A long rain fell that night and in the morning the autumn woods dripped a cold gloom. I didn't really want to leave my fireplace. Radiant heat permeates October strains and I was sore.

"I think we should try the pines and higher ground by the ski lodge. What do you think Meg?" asked Ted. Meg squealed and shimmied. He had arrived recharged and damn near full of glee again.

"OK but I can't hunt seven hours like yesterday." I tried not to seem jaded or in need of analgesics.

"No, no. I want to get home this afternoon and try a cover out by Lake Michigan. Might be some early flight birds there after this weather." These redheads were dangerous I noted to myself.

I wasn't sure what we were up to, but the idea of hunting in the almost arid terrain of red pines seemed simultaneously hopeful and stupid. Even I knew woodcock and grouse didn't care for the sterility and public atmosphere of red pine plantations. We started in a fringe of tall aspen buffered by an uneven strip of hemlock, maple, and oak. In a blur Meg pointed three woodcock and Ted and Bill each made good shots. It is one of the special pleasures of bird hunting to be unable to see number 8 or 9 shot leave your gun—or someone else's—and travel toward a target. The Borgeld brothers will never know that I missed the third woodcock flying through the powerline opening by, shall we say, the better part of an acre.

We hadn't quite reached the pines when Meg's bell abruptly fell silent to my left. I easily located her bent into a crooked L-shape. She was looking directly toward me. Those amber vizsla eyes glared right through me, almost in disgust! What had I done wrong? "Where's the bird, Meg, where's the bird?" I chattered stupidly. The intolerance of a bird dog's eyes is a wonderful sight.

Then I saw it move. That terrestrial cousin of the echinoderms, the giant land urchin, stood its ground a few feet beyond Meg. I was going to see something now, I was sure.

"Ooh, a flash point!" Ted arrived only slightly concerned, making a pickle face. "Meg doesn't like these guys, do you Meg? A lot of hunters shoot porcupines but I don't know…"

"Why would anyone do that?" I snapped back. "Hell, they belong out here more than we do." My habit of instant sanctimony came back to me faster than a porky's step.

"I agree, let's go Meg—find us a bird!" Ted commanded his lieutenant. The porcupine was now knee-high up a red maple trunk; its cream and black quills appeared to be the stuff of which very bad dreams are made.

I finished that outing and that season as a tourist of two worlds: hunting calmly behind another man's experienced dog, and thrashing, poking, and slogging through every kind of tangled, aspenish, bushy covert (I was proud of my bloodied hands and forearms—Red Badges of birding courage only a few good men would understand) northern Michigan has to offer.

It was a life.

· · · · ·

In September I met the Egg. It was probably just in time. Without the Egg, changes in weather, fluctuations in woodcock populations, and the ever-mysterious Grouse Cycle—always at its very nadir according to local biologists and sages—might not have been enough to save me from concluding that bird hunting wasn't much of a challenge for real sportsmen. Could insouciance and upland smugness have been far behind? And wouldn't the deepest of disillusionment have followed when reality came to call?

The Egg was real. An unlikely nickname for a Brittainy spaniel, to be sure, but nonetheless another man's dog that taught me powerful—if incomplete—lessons about grouse behavior, days in the field, and the demons of the human mind.

The Egg did not like to touch her lips to dead woodcock, did not care to listen to her master's commands even if he was about to lose his voice to permanent laryngeal hemorrhaging by screaming, and cooly disdained hunting within the same bioregion as her owner. What the Egg did love was running to daylight. To cover, through cover, and to the point. And holding woodcock until the next month if they agreed to stay. They didn't.

Sure the owner was a friend of mine and Ted's brother Bill, and sure it was great to get together in the crisp autumn air suffused with summer and winter and eternity, and sure the Egg earned a bird here and there, but damn it, all this yelling, this dog hunting, and this busting of precious grouse into the great beyond was wearing on me. It wasn't sporting.

Hunting behind Meg had always been so predictable, so Pavlovian that the world seemed inhuman, organized, and sensible. Now a roly-poly agent of chaos was turning the hunt into a frenetic chamber of dark thoughts, missed opportunities, and frayed psyches. I just wanted to greedily shoot a few birds behind a reliable dog, the Egg's owner simply wanted his dog to do anything that would prevent his emotional breakdown and estrangement from friends and family, and the Egg yearned to be released to the glorious and uncontrolled pursuit of certain scents.

I was upset with being upset. I was thinking of trying to point birds myself—then maybe I'd have a shot. I'm sure the Egg's owner knew I selfishly resented his dog's juvenile behavior and his bellowing at her to come back to the same hemisphere we were hunting, but I didn't know what to do or say. So I damned the Egg with faint praise, told myself that she must just be an exception to the rule, and promised that I would not fall victim to the ownership of such a confused animal. I made an oath to never indulge in pleadful ranting while afield should I ever own another bird dog. I hunted alone near home even more and developed a secret smugness about finishing the latter part of the season as the star in *The Loneliness of the Long Distance Hunter.*

· · · · ·

Oh, I'd like to tie that little ghost to a tree so she'd have to helplessly listen to me blaze away at grouse, I mumbled to myself. My partner, the owner of the dog (a thirty-five-pound comet of an English setter named Ginger) blowing toward the next county on the hot wind of desire, didn't seem to be the proper audience for sharing this thought. This was yet another angling friendship that had pleasantly evolved afield.

Then again, I couldn't hold back forever and finally broached the dreaded subject of so much interest to so many hunters: the behavior of someone else's dog—*your* dog—in the field. Actually, that's a euphemistic phrasing isn't it? What I really mean to say is the incompetent, impulsive, juvenile, stupid, inexplicable, and maniacal mistakes your dog has committed that helped to ruin what could have been a perfectly wonderful hunt.

"She's just far-ranging. That's the way setters like to work. It's their style," my partner and at this point still my friend replied, emphasizing the last word. I concluded that our friendship was much more valuable than any number of prematurely flushed grouse, and was relieved that he had not taken offense. I don't believe there's a single bird hunter of any substance who hasn't witnessed or at least heard of a friendship or family relationship that was strained or somehow turned into a stew of resentment because of a bird dog.

"Doesn't your dog work that way?" he asked evenly. My new dog, a German shorthair named Claire, was of course another subject altogether.

"She's got a lot to learn," I said with absolutely no sense of irony. In the setter I had met yet another culture. And I was struggling with intolerance. This white flash was not a nose-to-the-ground relative of the hound, not a Versatile that works close to its master, but rather a high-prancing speed merchant searching the air for the shadow of a scent. We would have to follow, not direct her. Where we, or at least I—myopically of course—wanted to look was based on the limitation of sight and held no significance. My friend mentioned something tongue-in-cheek about the setter being a Refined Breed.

That may explain how something—a prehistoric odor rising from pasty black soil or huge aspens leaning at dangerous angles over bushes and burdock taller than we were—in the narrow cover along the Sturgeon River that day seemed very wrong for a fleet English setter and two professional types to be hunting. We had been exploring a sunny ridge and followed a grouse through an opening down into a darkened theater of swift river, wind-thrown trees, and foreboding. Instead of shafts of sunlight illuminating the surroundings, the autumn light only heightened the dark bars of shadow everywhere around us. There are dead people in here from long ago, I told myself. "Something bad happened down in there" my friend offered later while still wiping his dog's blood off his hands. Like unpretentious boys and with no deliberation, we named the site the Valley of Death.

But there were grouse that day—thunderous, old gray birds that disappeared into shawls of Virginia creeper or vanished among fallen timber and black root masses the size of abandoned cabins. While my partner pressed on toward the general location of a flushed bird but especially toward the old railroad tracks and open daylight, I pulled and pushed my way through the webs of creeper and looked for a glimpse of Ginger. She moved like a pale fox through the Valley and disappeared for what seemed to me to be inappropriate periods of time. I yelled to the tracks that I had no idea of her location and then had to gulp a breath to correct myself. I saw movement in the waist-high weeds and bushes just forty feet or so to my right. I even heard the bell. Then more muffled ringing and more rustling. "She's hot!" I yelled and kicked my way forward as quickly as I could. "Are you coming in?" I was told to take the bird myself. I accepted but was still a little confused by the movements in front of me. This dog held points with smooth determination; she was not a creeper.

I shouted that she must have a running grouse and then broke through the final fence of vines to reach the point. The dog was either guarding or regarding a porcupine that looked to be the size of a bear cub. I did not have time to invoke déjà vu: this dog took a big bite.

In a burst of hysteria I wailed descriptions from the edge of the Valley and lunged into the fray. The round dark mammal wasn't in a hurry. The lithe white mammal squealed ever so faintly, began to show portions of red, and hopped unnaturally on three legs. One front leg was cushioned with quills. I think I feared for her eyes but I can't remember for sure. An unwelcome memory returned to me: the dazed, lost, and I believe dying bird dog wandering along a county road one day as I drove home from fishing the Sturgeon River. For miles I thought about turning around to help but continued on toward home. I grasped Ginger by the collar and pulled her through obstacles and up the eight feet of ballast onto the tracks. Her muzzle and throat were darted with quills. I was in a terrible state of mind.

What happened next was simple, instructive, and invaluable. My friend calmly (under the circumstances) reached into his vest, pulled out a hemostat, and proceeded to remove whole clumps of porcupine from his dog's face, leg, mouth, and throat. Within a few minutes the bleeding subsided nicely, I began to compose myself, and Ginger seemed to be looking back toward the Valley for more.

"No, that's it for today buddy," he said and began to wipe the blood from his hands. "I wouldn't go anywhere without a pair of these," he added as he wiped the surgical tool clean. For once I hardly had anything to say except that I was amazed the dog's eyes were unharmed and her behavior nearly normal except for a distinct limp.

We turned our backs to the Valley and walked to the trestle near our car. My responsibility—family, financial, emotional—and involvement in this crisis was over. And I felt completely drained.

"They're tough, they're different," he added as he picked up his dog and carried her across the river trestle.

"This was not an easy hunt," I said to no one in particular.

· · · · ·

Life, as I was indicating to the surgeon not long ago, is an evolving history. My shorthair shows great potential but is still unfinished. I am still unfinished. Yet the seasons and our dogs, young and old, press on.

I seem to recall that Ortega y Gasset observed that hunting dogs are like arrows, living extensions of the hunter. The grouse and bird dog fanatic from Leelanau County called one day in early March to ask if I would like a German shorthair. My friend knew my springer, knew about a particularly black birthday five years earlier, and I think even knew that on that day I was called back by my veterinarian's office an hour after our dog had been killed. The vet was running late with appointments and since I wanted a lab analysis—some kind of an explanation for the psychotic episodes—could I please take the specimen to the airport in time for the flight to Lansing and Michigan State University? I somehow agreed and rode the box on the seat next to me as if it were strontium 90. It was my dog's head.

"I don't know, you've taken me by surprise."

"That's the idea. You've seen Cochise."

Indeed I had seem him hunt on a couple of occasions in the hilly thickets near Lake Leelanau. What I saw was a fierce, animate arrow. He was sometimes a garbage-stealing, boneheaded whiner at home, but in the field Cochise was a sagacious incarnation of his master's hands. The litter had been sired by a dog with heart and power. I knew nothing of the female, except her owners once lived in Australia, and I didn't care.

"Thanks, I'll come and take a look."

Grouse and woodcock hunting are too enjoyable and the aroma of grilling woodcock (rare please) and lemon-butter grouse is far too medicinal to be sacrificed for check-cords, whistles, and backyard training regimens. In other words my shorthair, Claire, didn't get any time afield until her second fall.

During the bleak days of her first winter I watched the dog and our young daughter warm each other and our home. I reminded myself not to be harsh or punitive with either one. Positive reinforcement. No yelling.

Claire hit her first season running and showed great interest in ferns, popple thickets, vine-strewn windfall entanglements, and extending the distance between her heat-seeking course and me. She was on a mission but disdained her orders. Still, she handled some woodcock quite nicely and brought in a crippled grouse one day. I only exhorted her to hunt with me a couple of dozen times and slapped her with *No!* a few more.

Much to her dismay, I left her behind on hunts with friends and other dogs. It just didn't seem to be good form to subject them to our developing relationship. And I'd be damned if I was going to be the one to obliterate a good hunt with a goddamned lunatic of a dog. There was another problem. My friends' dogs knew the significance of wire; but Claire did not regard it at all. Wire is thick cobweb, wire is to run through. In lower Michigan nearly all public land meets the barbed wire of private property. I was certain that she would destroy an eye (*Daddy what did you do to Claire!*) or at least require zipper-length stitches if I ran her with the other dogs.

The leaves of that autumn turned brown and ocher and suddenly dense woods revealed long views of steely light. Snow propelled the last woodcock south and some days my dog ran with them. She apparently delighted in flushing grouse before I could see them, although I really don't know since I wasn't open to delight. Some people "put up" their antique cars, farm machinery, and various boats for the winter. I put up my dog and hunted the last woodcock and late grouse season alone again.

In the ensuing years it became obvious that weather isn't the only natural force that is unpredictable. Some hunts were marvels of blue sky, good dog work, and clean shooting. Later the house would fill with steam saturated with Worcestershire sauce, butter and acorn squash. Woodcock and Merlot. Grouse and a fine Riesling.

Other trips—near home or seventy-five miles away, it didn't seem to matter—were wicked mixtures of greyhound imitations, obscene epithets, and sulkathons in which the winner was the first one to discover a bird to chase. Alone.

Ready To Go
by Edmund Henry Osthaus (German-American, 1858–1928)

Artwork courtesy of the William Secord Gallery, New York, NY 10021

All of the great pine and hardwood forests of Michigan have been gone for a century. Some of the cleared land is still partially open and, of course, bordered by second and third-generation trees. I hunt a piece of state-owned land near my home that is remarkably large, interspersed with grassy, wild cherry openings, and punctuated with bird cover. For some reason—possibly because were are always alone—my dog often behaves herself and hunts with some of the purchase of her father.

We entered some misshapen circles of blackberry, aspen, and witch hazel after a good one-hour hunt in a different cover that I ended by throwing a temper tantrum and screaming myself hoarse. Claire had found and held three woodcock, two of which I shot as if I had handled a shotgun since puberty. The third bird I missed because it rose into a ceiling of bigtooth aspen leaves and disappeared. Not to worry. My dog followed up on the bird—or was it another?—again and again, and yes, probably again. Order surrendered to chaos and reason to rage.

I pursued the dog, my voice failing and croaking, for a heated distance. After a passionate reunion and simpering contrition, we rode together to another portion of the state land in silence.

I pulled off a two-track and parked in the edge of a field. I left her in the car while I retied my boots, combed the sweat out of my hair, and adjusted my sodden shirt and vest. If I were wearing a tie, I would have retied the knot.

I finally opened the door and commanded the dog to heel. She stopped nearby and looked up at me. Good enough. Trying to hone my voice into a flashing razor, I again confided my deepest desire: I want you to hunt *with me.*

She worked the first aspen and berry island thoroughly, checking back with me a couple of times, but there were only old splashes. She crossed an opening and faded into some birdy-looking bushes and trees. I had to let her range a little, but in less than a minute an uneasy near-silence stopped me. Claire's bell was quiet but when I closed the distance between her approximate location to my west, I immediately saw that she had ranged into maple and large timber. If there were any birds in there, they were chickadees and crows.

Her screams were not blood-curdling but instead muffled with blood. I don't know if she had sampled the porcupine from various angles or simply opened once wide and hard. I was a half-mile from my truck and many miles from the nearest people. Claire's keening shocked me in a way I had never known: this pain was mine, my dog was wounded.

I barely glanced at the porcupine as I rushed her out of the darkening woods into the light of open land. Her throat and muzzle gleamed red. My hands were already slippery with blood.

Her eyes were unharmed. I reached into my vest pocket and grasped the hemostat. I worked frantically on the quills under the chin, in her muzzle, and ominously protruding from her chest. Only a few had speared her legs and they were especially easy to remove, but why wasn't she calming down? Her jaws rattled together and deep whimpering poured from her throat. I pried open her mouth and would have run away through the field if I could. Blood spit from her tongue and the roof of her mouth was not visible through the dozens of stout quills. My forearms were red as I fought off panic. By the time I finished removing what I could, she had suddenly calmed down and stopped crying. Her bleeding almost disappeared and on my rush back to the truck she veered toward a little aspen island to start hunting again!

I drove back dirt roads at improper speeds and thought of what I had once told an acquaintance who was thinking of bringing a bird dog into the family. "If I were to give you one, which was once done for me, I'd say this: 'There's a little bit of blood with one of these but they're almost as wonderful as daughters and sons.'"

Now, fairly drenched in the family dog's blood, I wasn't so sure of anything. I poured on the speed and turned up the radio. "To All the Girls I've Loved Before" reverberated in the cab and suddenly flashing past my eyes was more than a blur of northern maple, aspen, and pine. All of the easy, carefree hours behind Meg, Ginger, and Chelsea the Egg rushed through my blood and then focused. I owed them and my friends everything. So it's to those white and porky and auburn canine girls who gave me more pleasure than I was capable of realizing that I dedicate this long song.

Steve Grooms *grew up in central Iowa at a time when even inept hunters without dogs could find plenty of pheasants. He moved to Minnesota when pheasants were so scarce that hunters without dogs rarely saw one. That led him to buy his first hunting dog, beginning the fourteen-year adventure told in his story, "Pirates." Grooms lives in St. Paul, Minnesota, with his wife, daughter, and two hunting dogs. The family spends as much time as possible at their cabin on the shores of Lake Superior, near Cornucopia, Wisconsin. Grooms is a freelance writer. His books include* Modern Pheasant Hunting, Pheasant Hunter's Harvest, Bluebirds!, The Cry of the Sandhill Crane, The Ones That Got Away, *and* The Return of the Wolf.

PIRATES

by Steve Grooms

Last night I brought out our film projector, blew the dust off it and spooled up the film Kathe shot the day we met Brandy. Because our old Super 8 camera had no microphone, the film is eerily silent. The only noise one hears as the film rolls is the rattle of the projector itself. Dogs bark, people laugh, shotguns fire...all in pantomime. In the darkness of my basement room, jittery frames of film pour out their flow of softly focused images like a dream.

In the film, a man throws a stick across the snowy parking lot of a northwoods resort. A mob of rotund springer pups surges hither and yon, fighting over that trophy stick. It looks like they are playing rugby. The man keeps throwing the stick. Finally there is just one puppy in the film. The camera whirls giddily to show the rest of the little spaniels monkeyballed together in exhaustion in their straw bed. While they sleep off their exertions, their aggressive sister continues to chase the stick, again and again.

I have trouble now recognizing myself in the slim, dark-haired youth in that silent film. But I have no trouble recognizing Brandy. Indeed, it was all there to be seen, had I then only possessed eyes that could see: what she was, what she would become, what she and I would be together, the agony and glory of it all.

What is missing in that film is the mentor I should have brought along to advise me, the veteran hunter who would have told me, "Son, let me speak as clearly as possible: you don't know jack shit about dogs. That little springer is way too much dog for you. Hell, she's too hot for most professional trainers." But as I said, that wise man was not there the day of the filming, just a young fool who had already fallen in love with the high-spirited puppy he soon would name Brandy.

Back then there was an empty lot behind a post office not far from our St. Paul home. It is part of a shopping mall now, of course, but in the early 1970s about a dozen pheasants scratched out a living in that vacant urban lot. On winter afternoons when my college classes were over, I took little Brandy out among the snow, weeds, and broken wine bottles of the vacant lot. She and I would hack about until we managed to spook up the pheasants. As they clattered into the sky, I would leap about like a kangaroo with a hotfoot and howl, "Birds! *Birds! Brandy, get the birds!*" And this, I blush to report, was all I did to "train" my young dog to hunt.

Had I known anything about dogs—anything at all—I would have realized Brandy's blood already boiled with bird lust. Even I should have recognized that my challenge as a trainer was to gain some degree of control over my hotheaded puppy. But in my towering ignorance, I thought I had to teach her to care about birds. My training amounted to pouring gas on the white-hot embers of Brandy's innate birdiness.

Brandy was five months old when Kathe and I took her to observe a springer field trial. We had some vague notion this might be educational for her. Apart from our bizarre romps behind the post office, Brandy had no experience with birds. She had never had her mouth on one. The only field command she knew was *Get the birds!* She had never heard a gun. In spite of all that, and in defiance of common sense, I allowed myself to be talked into entering Brandy in the puppy stakes.

At a signal from the judges, I told Brandy—what else?—to *Get the birds!* Amazingly, she quartered naturally. Brandy found and flushed the first pigeon within seconds. When the gunner touched off a short magnum 12-gauge load right over her head, Brandy was too preoccupied marking the fall of the bird to mind the muzzle blast. On her own, she decided to pick up the dead pigeon and bring it back to me, just as if we had rehearsed this act a thousand times. Her work on the second pigeon was similarly perfect. Alas, Brandy's third pigeon had been dizzied too vigorously when the bird boy stuck it in the grass. That bird flew away woozily just a few feet above the grass. When the gunner missed it, Brandy continued racing along under the pigeon until she was finally stopped by a tight fence a quarter of a mile away. That mad dash cost Brandy a blue ribbon, but she did take second place in what was to be our first and last field trial.

Brandy's subsequent career was to span geography from the Missouri to Ontario and from Wisconsin to Nebraska. In addition to various species of ducks and geese, Brandy and I hunted prairie chickens, sharp-tailed grouse, Hungarian partridge, quail, ruffed grouse, and woodcock. But above all, Brandy was a hunter of pheasants. Fittingly, her first rooster was memorable.

We had been hunting some scrubby brushland north of the Twin Cities. I had managed to bag a grouse and two or three woodcock. When we came upon a little marsh near a cornfield, Brandy rushed some cattails. Up came a turkey-sized old rooster, cursing like a truck driver stuck in traffic. He was so big and raucous I lost my composure and made a tentative shot that only broke a wing. When the rooster sailed into some bulrushes in about two feet of water, I rushed to the spot in knee-deep water and began shrieking for Brandy to help me find our bird. By ignoring me, she soon found the cock where he'd run, forty yards away. But then Brandy refused to retrieve him to me even after I'd walked over to her and stood three feet away, repeatedly demanding that she fetch the bird. I gave up after fifteen minutes of comic frustration and retrieved my soggy trophy myself.

That night I confessed my disappointment to Kathe. I explained that my little springer apparently lacked the strength to handle birds as big as pheasants. Just as I spoke, the doorbell rang. Among Brandy's idiosyncrasies was a compulsion to greet visitors with some precious object in her mouth. Out of the corner of my eye, I saw Brandy streak to the pile of birds in the kitchen. She kicked away the woodcock, pawed her way past the grouse, and seized that gorgeous rooster. When our friends walked in, Brandy paraded before them like a major domo, brandishing her rooster like a baton.

She obviously had enough muscle to carry the biggest pheasant ever born. So why had Brandy stonily refused to retrieve that same bird to me when I had been so close?

I finally understood, and with that comprehension I made progress toward understanding my quirky partner. In thirteen years of hunting with me, Brandy retrieved several hundred pheasants. She fetched many across rivers and through tangles of brush. She made several retrieves at distances I estimated at about half a mile. But she consistently refused to retrieve a bird whenever I stood close to her. In Brandy's view, if I was that near I could damn well walk two steps and pick the bird up myself. Brandy would do anything I asked of her, *if* she saw the point of it.

I made another key discovery about her character when we hunted Iowa for the first time. Kathe and I made that trip in December, right after Christmas. Seven weeks of heavy hunting pressure had made most of the surviving pheasants too jumpy to be approached. Kathe and I were able to get limits by hunting hard from sunup to sunset three days in a row, but it was exhausting work, especially for Brandy. I kept expecting her to give in to exhaustion, but every morning she was as full of ginger as she had been on the first day.

We were slowly working our way back toward Minnesota on the fourth day when I spotted a creek that had the thickest cover we had seen since entering Iowa. The creek was twisty and deeply eroded. Its banks were completely overgrown with horse weeds and willows, and its bottom was a tangled mat of marsh grasses. When I asked permission to hunt the place, the farmer broke into guffaws. "If you really want to go in *there* fella, you're more than welcome," he said, "but I'm tellin' you it's a waste of time. That cover's just too thick. Last week, six guys from Illinois went through there with three dogs, and they couldn't dig a single rooster out of all those weeds." He didn't see the furtive smile on my face as I headed back to the car.

Brandy flushed the first rooster from the willows on the south shore. Ten minutes later, she dug the second out of a thicket of horse weeds. Her third bird was a running cripple that couldn't run quite as fast as she. The fourth rooster ran for nearly a hundred yards on the high bank before Brandy caught up with him and boosted him into the sky. At my shot, he plunked down right on the frozen surface of the creek. Brandy dove off the bank to grab him. But when she tried to return she found herself confronting a sheer wall of black dirt that was about fourteen feet high and undercut near the top.

I knew she could never scramble up that wall even without the extra weight of the rooster, but I wanted to see what she would do. Brandy charged the wall three times, getting halfway up each time before gravity dragged her back. The loose soil of the bank simply could not give her madly spinning feet enough purchase to lift her. Without putting the rooster down, Brandy attacked the wall a fourth time. Her feet were a blur. Dirt clods and stones shot behind her in a torrent and went pinging off the ice of the river like birdshot. With agonizing slowness, her body inched higher and higher until she finally clawed her way over the edge.

As stupid as I was about hunting dogs back then, even I knew I had witnessed something astonishing. I had just seen a dog levitate herself by a ferocious act of will. I vowed to never underestimate her again.

That same will, over the next several years, was the glory and the agony of our hunts. Brandy hunted every moment of every day at a mad gallop, attacking the cover as if the fate of the world depended upon her shagging every bird out of it. She seemed to believe her sacred mission was to flush every bird before I could get close enough to do that myself.

It was generally a pure accident when I happened to be close enough to one of Brandy's flushes to take a desperate poke at the disappearing bird. In the grouse woods she ranged so far from me that the panicked birds sometimes flew toward me. I bagged a lot of grouse by pass-shooting birds that had no idea I was there. As much as she loved me, Brandy was mad for birds. She pursued them with maniacal energy and no regard to where I might be.

All my anguished efforts to bring Brandy under control failed. I screamed at her. I chased her. When I caught her, I beat her. That stopped when I realized the beatings were boring her. Brandy was utterly indifferent to pain. She regarded her beatings a waste of precious hunting time. When I finished thrashing her, Brandy would grin and go right back to hunting with her unique volcanic energy. After one particularly frustrating trip to Iowa, I told Kathe, "I have the worst hunting dog in the world. Her every effort is focused on flushing birds eighty yards ahead of me. She has the range of a pointing dog, only she doesn't point."

Something had to change, and I really didn't have much of a choice about what it would be. I loved bird hunting and Brandy too much to give up either one. By the time we'd put in two seasons together, I knew she was too aggressive to limit her range to the cover right around me. It was equally clear that all the bird action was happening where Brandy was. If I meant to shoot anything, I had to be somewhere near her. Since Brandy would not restrict her hunt to my proximity, I extended mine to join hers. That is a fancy way of saying I spent thirteen years running desperately in bird cover, looking less like a hunter than a man trying to catch a train that has just left the station ahead of him.

It wasn't pretty and it wasn't easy. Brandy was more fit and more fleet than I, and she didn't have to carry a shotgun. In all the years I hunted with her, my slowest pace was the fastest walk a young man can manage in heavy cover. Much of the time I had to trot, and often I gripped my shotgun like a track relay baton and simply lit out as fast as I could go.

On one typical full-tilt hunt, a friend who was chugging along beside me turned to say something. He found himself staring at the chainlink soles of my hunting boots. I had hit a wire fence at shin height, out of sight in the weeds. Because of my hurtling momentum, hitting the fence didn't knock me down but launched me into the air like a man shot out of a cannon.

Another time I was attempting to sprint through a swampy stand of willows because I could hear Brandy somewhere ahead of me putting up roosters. When I tripped on a hummock, my shotgun left my hands and flew thirty feet before impaling itself muzzle-first in the mud. The shotgun was sticking out of the ground like a spear when I retrieved it. I saw that about four inches of mud were packed in each barrel, and just then two of Brandy's roosters flew through an overhead opening in the willows. As the roosters flapped safely out of sight, I cursed my predicament in language that blistered bark off the nearest willows.

In spite of such moments, I became a specialist at hunting roosters in marshes because in such swampy cover I could stay slightly nearer Brandy than on firm ground. Grouse cover was the worst for us because it didn't slow Brandy down at all but tore me up considerably. I routinely ran into trees, frequently ricocheting off one or two before gathering control and plunging forward again. We hunted grouse with the desperate pace of two escapees from a chain gang.

Because of our strenuous hunting style, I wore a thin cotton shirt and light vest at times when everyone else was wearing wool shirts and insulated coats. Even then I sweated copiously as I stumbled along in Brandy's wake, my face a hunter orange. Once when a partner in Iowa made me stop so he could smoke a cigarette, I went into hypothermia. I used to wear out two pairs of boots each hunting season, and the nylon hunting pants I bought in September looked in December like they had been put through a food processor.

It was much the same for Brandy. She didn't know what discomfort was when hunting. Brandy was a dog who would hunt hard in sandburs. After several hunting trips, I found she had sustained cuts so deep I almost fainted when I found them, but she had given no sign of the pain. When she took a full hit in the face (and tongue, and lips, and gums) from a porcupine, Brandy merrily hunted all the way back to the car. For Brandy and me, upland hunting was a contact sport.

According to an old cliche, dogs and the people who own them come to resemble each other in appearance. It just isn't so. But Brandy and I came to resemble each other in a more fundamental way, namely our passionate and intemperate approach to hunting. In that, we were identical twins. We went out of our way to attack cover that normal hunters refused to enter. Our ferocious attack on bird cover was macho, enormously wasteful of energy and about as subtle as a chain saw.

We were twins in another sense. Not until Brandy had been dead two years did I finally understand a central fact about her. Brandy—*forgive me for saying this, old girl!*—had a mediocre nose. She hunted with cyclonic energy because that was her nature and because she simply needed to cover a great deal of ground to make contact with hot scent. Dogs with sensitive noses can trail cold scent until it becomes a hot flush. Not Brandy. Cold scent just confused her, so Brandy had no choice but to rip around in bird cover until she made a smoking hot contact. For my part, I lacked any sense of where a bird might be found. We were quite a duo: a dog with a cold nose and a man who didn't know what he was doing. Yet we each compensated for our deficiency by hunting so long and hard we found birds in spite of ourselves.

So it went for five desperate years while I waited for Brandy to get old, mellow, and slow. That didn't happen. But while Brandy could do nothing to improve her nose, she could improve her head. In her sixth and seventh years, Brandy become extraordinarily effective by applying all the lessons she had learned in her first years. It was fascinating to watch her at work; you could see the gears turning. If Brandy and another dog were looking for a running pheasant, the other dog would rely upon its nose while Brandy would draw upon the prodigious data bank of bird behavior between her ears. Time after time, the dog with the bum nose and the bird smarts was first to come up with the prize.

Just when Brandy should have been aging toward the decline that inevitably drags down all bird dogs, she hit her peak. The years she was eight, nine, ten, and eleven were the stuff of legends. While our hunting style was still queer and grossly inefficient, Brandy and I had become an exceptionally effective team. We always sought out the most difficult walking, down in the slop of marshes and the mazes of young willows. Since Brandy and I hunted twice as fast as anyone who might be with us, we always took one end of the line and worked a huge zig-zag pattern so we covered twice as much ground as our partners. People often told me we hunted too fast. Yet in all those years, I don't remember anybody finding a rooster in ground we had just covered.

A hunt from Brandy's ninth year typifies our partnership at its peak. We left home about noon to join friends for a five-day South Dakota trip. When I crossed the state line there was a little legal shooting time left. I stopped at a gas station to ask the owner if he knew of a marsh in the area with so much heavy cover that it couldn't be hunted. He did. In that marsh, Brandy flushed two roosters and caught a running cripple just before sunset. We then hunted three days in the Platte area, getting three-bird limits each day, thanks mostly to Brandy.

On our fifth morning, she and I hunted alone in the largest wildlife management area in the state. The first cock Brandy found there took us on a wild gallop across the prairie and through two separate cattail marshes before it ran out of options and had to fly. We chased the second rooster right through the heart of the marsh before Brandy caught up with him. While she was retrieving him, she ran smack into the third pheasant. We returned to the car with three handsome roosters, having hunted half an hour.

We were back in Minnesota, heading home, when I realized we were near a swampy Minnesota wildlife management area that was an old favorite of ours. I reached it with less than an hour left of legal shooting time. Brandy only needed half that time to find and flush a Minnesota limit of two roosters for me.

Please don't misunderstand. I am not boasting about how many birds we could kill in those days. What I am trying to convey is the confidence—call it cockiness—I came to feel each day we entered the field. I had spent five years fearing I had the worst dog in the world. I then savored six years of a remarkably effective and joyous partnership. As Brandy got better each year, I began to believe she had found a way to transcend the laws of aging.

The first intimations of mortality came on a South Dakota Sioux reservation near the mighty Missouri River. In that year of pheasant superabundance it should have been easy to come home with our party limit of forty-five pheasants. But my partners were not shooting well. Not to put too fine a point on it, Kathe and Jerry were each burning up a box of shells for each rooster they bagged, which meant the dogs had to flush that many more birds. Brandy hunted with her usual ferocity for five days in temperatures better suited for sunbathing than chasing footloose roosters. In that time she probably flushed between four hundred and five hundred pheasants, counting hens, and she retrieved about forty roosters.

Finally, we needed one bird to fill our limit. Brandy put up two roosters, and Jerry broke a wing on one of them. Brandy ran to the fall but did not come back. We found her staring quizzically down a badger hole, and I guessed Jerry's cock had scooted down there. Brandy was always so fond of digging we used to joke there must have been a backhoe somewhere in her family tree. I pointed down the hole and said the magic words: "Get the bird!" Dirt began to fly. After fifteen minutes, Brandy's whole body was below ground, with just the backs of her legs still in sight. (We have a photo of this.) It was obviously hopeless, so I called her back. Brandy wriggled out of her hole and turned to present me with a face comically loaded with black dirt. But she had a single rooster tail feather in her teeth. I sent her back down to finish the job.

When we had Jerry's bird, we set off walking back to the car. But I had a panicky, amorphous feeling of something being wrong. Then I understood: Brandy was *following* me. She hadn't been behind me since she was six months old. After five days of ferocious hunting in that heat, and almost half an hour of vigorous tunneling, Brandy had hit her limit. She looked embarrassed, and she soon got out ahead of me again. But in that moment I realized that even Brandy could not defy the processes of aging forever. She was eleven at the time.

One year later, Brandy still slashed through the cover with vigor and efficiency, outperforming all the dogs who shared the field with her. But that was the year Brandy and I plunged recklessly into an icy swamp that nearly claimed our lives. As I struggled against exhaustion and hypothermia that night, dragging behind me the old dog whose body had locked up tight like a statue in that cold water, I had a lot of time to contemplate the fact our partnership was nearing its end. I realized that night that if I lived to hunt again, I had to find and begin training the younger dog who would eventually replace Brandy.

Brandy's thirteenth year was amazingly strong. I could tell she had slowed down a little, but anyone else would have complained that she was roaring around out of control like any damnfool puppy. In a hellish phragmites marsh in Minnesota, Brandy found a running rooster that evaded three other dogs. She hunted heroically in an Iowa blizzard in December that left the cover full of dead birds, their beaks or feathers impacted with frozen snow.

Brandy declined tragically in her fourteenth year. By then she was deaf, nearly blind, arthritic and weak from lack of exercise. She was also riddled with cancer, although I did not know that for some time. I mostly hunted with her young replacement, leaving the old warrior to bark in frustration as she saw me leaving home dressed in the hunting garb she knew so well. I was afraid she'd get lost if I took her into the field with little vision, no hearing, and a poor sense of smell to bring her back to me.

At last I realized her career was winding to an end. In a "Masterpiece Theater" series running at that time, a father decides to buy his dying son a date with a prostitute. In much the same sense, I decided to buy my dying partner a trip to a game farm. By luck, the birds that the owner put out for us were the prettiest and wildest pen-raised pheasants I have ever encountered. Just a year earlier, Brandy and I hunted the same field. On that day, the preserve had released six birds, and Brandy had found seven of them.

The miracle I had irrationally expected did not occur. Time after time for thirteen years, I had seen the sight of weeds magically restore Brandy when it seemed she was surely too footsore, cut-up, and exhausted to hunt again. Time after time

I had seen her rise, phoenix-like, to assault the cover again. Foolishly, I had expected it to happen one more time.

But although Brandy tried her hardest, she was over-matched. Three times I saw her bump into weeds that knocked her off her feet with their springy resistance. She did manage to frighten several pheasants into flight. And one, a hen, she retrieved to me, pausing three times along the way to drop it and pant in exhaustion.

Then she got on the trail of a cock I could see sprinting down a cornrow ahead of us. Brandy's last rooster was a magnificent bird with a tail in the twenty-inch range. Brandy bustled eagerly along on his trail, snuffling frantically to suck in enough scent to tell her which way to go. The pheasant was just too quick for her. He reached the end of the row and turned the corner. I saw he would get away unless I ran at him to force a flush. But he wasn't my bird; he was Brandy's. And he had beaten her. Though I had already paid for this rooster, I knew I didn't have the right to kill him.

Brandy neither heard nor saw the bird when he flushed. Cackling with indignation, he sailed to the protection of some trees beyond a dark little river. Brandy snuffled around in confusion when she reached the spot he'd flushed from. With stinging eyes, I picked her up and carried her to the car.

Three months later, Brandy made her own passage across a dark river.

I think I now understand that bird dogs can be great in four specific ways. Three are based in natural ability: nose, heart, and intelligence. Some dogs also excel in what I've called "manners," which is how well they have been trained. With reason, veteran dog men reserve their highest regard for those rare dogs that excel in all four areas.

Yet I treasure the memory of a dog who was highly imperfect. Brandy had no manners—which was my fault—and not much more nose. In spite of that, she managed to elevate herself to a kind of greatness through courage and sheer will, much the way she once elevated herself up an impossible wall of undercut soft dirt. I can't believe any dog ever accomplished more with the gifts he or she was given than Brandy.

Although I know it is foolish, I sometimes wish the wisdom of my graying head could be installed in the resilient young body I once possessed. More realistically, I wish I could have known even a little about birds and dogs back when Brandy and I first met. But time is a river that runs only one way. One becomes wise by being foolish first, and Brandy and I were good at that. I guess most dog men have regrets about their first hunting dog.

Yet any regrets I have are trivial when set next to all the fond memories that linger of our unique partnership. I have written two books and scores of articles about my adventures with Brandy, and many stories remain to be told. After all, we had almost a decade and a half together, and those were prodigious years. I don't know how a man ever stops missing a dog like that.

Brandy represents a whole lusty era of my life, a time that is now gone just as permanently as is Brandy. We were a pair of pirates, Brandy and I, two bird-mad swashbucklers who flailed at the sport with dull broadswords and stormed into places where prudent folk never go. I can never again be the person I was with Brandy. And this is part of what we say goodbye to when we bury a dog: a part of ourselves.

Randy Lawrence made his first trip west for sharp-tailed grouse in 1991 and since then, divides his autumns between being on the prairies and wishing he were there. A close friend who manages his farm for quail and dog training introduced Lawrence to hunting off horseback. "I've always envied the pros who head for Saskatchewan to run bird dogs in the late summer through the early part of the season," says Lawrence, who has kept Tennessee Walking horses as an important companion pleasure to his Longhunter setters and pointers. "It's everything I dream about the rest of the year: a steady pony, the dogs sailing across big country, pretty points, big covey rises, and elegant wingshooting. To me, it's the ultimate expression of the gun dog experience."

Closer to home, there are bobwhites, ruffed grouse, and woodcock within minutes of the Hocking College campus in Nelsonville, Ohio, where Randy is a teacher of writing. First published in The Drummer *in 1986, his work has since appeared in* Gray's Sporting Journal, Game and Gun, Shooting Sportsman, Quail Unlimited, *and* The Double Gun Journal. *He is currently a field editor for* Sporting Clays Magazine. *Randy, his wife, Jacklyn, and their four children share a Lancaster, Ohio, home with three bird dogs, one yellow Labrador, and an insolent Jack Russell terrier.*

RING THE BELL FOR POPEYE

by Randy Lawrence

Old Popeye had gone down hard, and he wasn't getting up. Tom Roberts stared, slack-jawed, from the other side of the white board fence, the shotgun and bird dog forgotten.

Roberts had bustled through breakfast, thinking he would give the pointer a long hunt on the back edge of the farm. An ice-blue dawn promised the first bright weather in a week, and he meant to have all of it.

While he worked his feet into the scarred pair of birdshooters, he opened and closed his right eye, gravely testing the left. He was still suspicious, though only a tinge of blur remained. For Tom Roberts, most matters came down to trust, and that Judas eye had let him down. No body part should ever betray a fellow during the bird season.

In the back porch mudroom, Roberts spilled a handful of purple shells into one deep pocket of the faded canvas vest. While he fumbled for his whistle and reached the battered shotgun down off the wall pegs, he peeked out the storm door to see his "house covey" scuttling around a feeder set in the winter ruins of his garden. The quail melted off into tall weeds when Roberts popped open the porch door and stepped out into the morning.

He fetched Holly, fat from a season of inactivity, down from the kennels and was trudging past the barn when he noticed Popeye drowsing in the pale January sunlight. Roberts did not want to startle him, coming up on the horse's blind side that way, so he gestured for the pointer to hold and called softly to the ancient white gelding.

"Hey, Ol' Man. Hey, Popeye!"

As if he'd been hit by an electric prod, Popeye squealed, tossed his head, then leaped high, twisting and kicking. He piled into the frost-steeled paddock dirt, struggled to free his legs, then went limp. The thick white neck flopped, slamming the horse's head into the turf.

Roberts backed away, horrified. What had he done? Trying not to panic, he collected the tail-tucked Holly and huffed back up to the kennel shed. Tom penned the dog, leaned the empty shotgun in the corner next to the feed bin, and, from habit, dug the heavy calf's bell out of his vest pocket and hung it over a nail amid a dozen faded field trial ribbons. He felt light-headed, and stumbled back to the shed's doorway.

Slumped against the casing, Roberts could look down into the paddock. Popeye lay stretched and still, like the last mound of dirty snow left in a slow thaw. Tom closed his eyes and tried to catch his breath, tried to beat down the sick feeling roiling in his belly.

What else could happen this year? In October, he'd lost
'Lilah, the setter, to cancer. November brought problems with
his own health, a bad cold that had sunk into pleurisy. The
coughing came from so deep in Tom's chest that the retina tore
loose in his left eye during one wrenching, hacking fit. There
had been surgery, then another six weeks stolen from his
shooting.

"Tween that old horse and me, we ain't got but one
head's worth of good eyes," he joked when his nephews came to
visit. For the first time in his life, Tom Roberts had needed to
ask a neighbor for help with his chores.

And now this. He stayed propped in the doorway until the queasiness ebbed, then walked down the hill again, this time to the tack room he'd made out of the barn's old milkhouse. Through the warm smells of harness and horses, he found the moldy, leather halter Popeye had worn lately only for his Amish farrier.

The horse was barely breathing, squeezing air in shallow, choking rasps. His head was flat to the ground, his left eye topside, brimming with hurt and blinking against the sunlight. Roberts knelt and gently worked the halter up and over Popeye's ears. The cheekpiece buckled easily.

Clucking quietly, as if urging him up a steep and slippery grade, Tom slid his hand around the noseband and leaned back in a steady pull.

"C'mon, Popeye. Get on up!"

The horse made no effort to move. Roberts let off for a moment, gathered himself, and dug his boot heels in for another try.

"Come *on,* goddammit! Get *up*!"

Popeye made a throaty moan, but only his head gave to Roberts's weight.

Tom dropped the halter and sank back on his haunches. A seizure? Some kind of stroke? Had Popeye just been startled, then hurt himself in the fall? He stroked the soft muzzle and felt warm breath on his palm.

A shiver rippled along the horse's ribs, and Roberts felt a chill climb his own neck. Popeye. Never sick. Never tired. Just old. Finally, just too damned old.

Tom had retired him from hunting the year before. He didn't know exactly how old Popeye was, but he had ridden him for over twenty years. Last season, Roberts had begun to notice him laboring up hills he'd always taken easily, stumbling over ground that didn't seem rough. The day Popeye tripped at the shallow creek ford and went to his knees, Tom had kicked himself out of the stirrups and made a clumsy vault into fast water.

Roberts had staggered back to fish for the reins, feeling the wet cold creep through his boots and brush pants while Popeye found his footing and shook himself like a giant white dog. Tom led him out of the creek, whistled for 'Lilah, then walked the long mile back to the barn. In a box stall deep with straw, he unsaddled Popeye and took an extra long time rubbing him down. There had been a month left in the quail season, but Tom pastured his horse and hunted February on foot.

The field trialer who had sold Popeye to Roberts swore the one-eyed gelding was out of a flashy, gaited mare by a registered Tennessee walking horse. But the squat build, the coarse head, the heavily-feathered fetlocks hinted at a less imperial ancestry, and Popeye had more bouncing rack to him than any kind of smooth, running walk.

That hadn't mattered to Roberts. He had been new to bird dogs and shooting ponies; the little horse was a calm, easy keeper. From Popeye's broad back, Tom Roberts went to school.

Late each summer, he would leave his farm implement dealership with a younger brother, load the pickup camper, and take ten weeks' vacation pulling a heavy trailer that fairly bowed at the axles: Popeye, a cache of gear, grain, and hay, and four bird dogs bound for the Canada prairies.

Some years, he hooked up with pro trainers he met at field trials, getting his own string worked in exchange for tending horses, scooping kennels, scouting, roading dogs into condition, whatever was needed.

Later on, he struck out on his own, finding farmers who would let him keep camp in the middle of good bird country. Alone with his horse and his dogs, Robert rode out after gray partridge and sharp-tailed grouse.

The Model 21 he'd shot since college stuffed in the saddle boot, Roberts would cast two dogs. His particular fancy was a mixed brace, setter and pointer, and he would whistle them into the wind before nudging Popeye into a nodding, plodding, all-day stride.

Sometimes, Tom sang to his dogs, calling, "Heeyy! Heeyyep! Yep, yep, heeyy!" to keep them hunting, to let them know where he was without their checking in.

Most days, though, he rode in silence, his eyes on white shapes tacking back and forth against the horizon's dark rim.

Settled into his trooper saddle's deep seat, he daydreamed to the creak of oiled leather, and faint jingle of dog bells.

When one of the distant forms finally froze, Tom would squeeze Popeye into a slow canter and, if he could, wave the other dog around in position to back. He usually rode within twenty or thirty yards of the stand, dismounted, and let the reins fall to the ground. Popeye would stand as quietly as if he were staked out, head cocked so his left eye faced the action, ears pricking forward and back while Roberts pulled the shotgun and watched his dogs.

In the early part of the season, sharptails held tight, sometimes ripping out of the ground only when Roberts stepped into the flock. On the rise, they made frantic chortle-cackles, and Tom would measure his shooting in deliberate, clean strokes.

The dogs fetched the big grouse gently, gray feathers barely ruffled in easy mouths. Studying each bird as if he'd never held one in hand before, Roberts would give the dogs a blow, then carefully arrange the grouse, head to tail, in the mesh game bag tied behind the saddle.

Partridge were tougher to pin, harder to shoot. Roberts had permission to gun huge tracts of farmland, and during the grain harvest, he and the dogs started spooky Huns from yellow stubble. Later, Popeye would trail the dogs to abandoned farm sites where partridge loafed in the shadows of ruined sheds and leaning grain bins. From ghost barnyards, the birds lifted with cries like rusty shutter hinges on tumbled-in, homesteaders' shanties.

Often the covey would flush before Roberts could reach his dogs. Broke steady to partridge temptation, they stood tall and trembling, eyes wide, marking the birds' long flight. The younger dogs always had to be bullied in to heel at Tom's stirrups before he could lead them away from the flush, get them under control, then whistle them on again.

Roberts stayed on the prairie, hunting wheatfield edges, the deep fingers of brushy coulees veining down through broken country, thick creek bottoms dressed in rosehip and buffalo berry. At dusk, he burned wrist-sized sticks of carefully hoarded deadfall into shimmering orange coals, roasting game on a homemade spit he faithfully tended until the birds were done to a turn.

He would lie stretched by the fire, propped on one elbow, letting the meat cool a bit before savoring each bite of sweet, dark sharptail breast, still pink near the bone. Tired dogs lay curled by their tie-outs, snoring off the day's hunt and a full feed pan. Popeye would be picketed off from the camp, the sound of his yellow teeth snatching at dry prairie grass, loud in the chill night air.

As the nights turned colder, Roberts would need an extra blanket in the camper, and the dogs slept double in snug kennel boxes built into the trailer. The morning he had to break more than a skim of ice in the water buckets, Tom would know that time was running short.

On the last day of his hunt, Tom would run all four dogs together. The goal was to get one obliging pack of grouse to hunker down and treat Roberts to the spectacle of four hard-muscled gun dogs together on one stand. Some years, it happened just that way, one or two dogs pointing, the rest stacked behind, honoring. Then after Tom had made a photograph or two from the saddle, he'd deliberately ride up the birds.

Popeye would arch his heavy neck and dance a little through the cackle and chaos of sharptail wings, the dogs holding while grouse faded into distant specks, their flap-flap-glide, flap-flap-glide, stroking them over the edge of another prairie autumn.

Back home in Kentucky, quail was the quarry, and Roberts hunted his own farm, plus several thousand acres of his neighbors' ground. After each morning's chores, he would ride to where he wanted to hunt, two dogs trotting alongside.

November was spent prospecting for new coveys, getting reacquainted with bevies of birds that he had hunted for years. The Winchester still rode along in the scabbard, but Roberts shot just enough quail to keep the dogs keen and the occasional evening meal a delight. Most of the covies he flushed in front of staunch dogs were saluted with blank popper shells Tom loaded himself.

Saturdays and Sundays, Popeye's saddlebags toted sandwiches and a canteen of sweet cider, and on warm days he would noon in the sun. One pointer and a setter would sit attentively next to him, trying desperately to be still, drool oozing from the sides of their mouths while they watched Roberts eat quail breast and thin slices of Vidalia onion pressed between home-made wheat bread. Sometimes he wrapped himself in his rain slicker and capped lunch with a short nap.

Usually, the dogs' fidgeting woke him. During noon breaks, he always threw the stirrup leathers over the saddle seat to keep Popeye from getting tangled in them and to remind himself to tighten the cinch. While he fussed with the tack, the setter and pointer would whirl and wriggle and whine, begging to go.

Finally, Tom would "whoa" them, lead Popeye away, then swing into the saddle. When it seemed they would fairly burst, Roberts would growl, "All right now, hunt 'em up", and watch twin streaks of bird dog burn up a long fencerow or reach out for a cedar-studded knoll bristling over the fields…

Over two hours had passed, and Popeye had not moved. Tom's legs were cramped. He heaved himself to his feet, let the blood come back, and limped into the barn for an armload of choice timothy hay and a bucket of fresh water that he arranged close by the horse's head. Roberts tried not to hear the halting, ragged breathing that now came almost as a sob.

When he could bear his vigil no longer, Tom stumped back to the house, brewed a pot of coffee, then let it grow cold on the kitchen counter while he sat near the window and stared off toward the paddock.

He thought about a time right after he'd retired the old horse. A friend had come from town, and they'd headed out with 'Lilah just above the kennels. It was the shank end of February, and Roberts had released some of the feisty, pen-reared birds he kept to hunt closer to home when the season waned. Rounding the hill above the far pasture, the guest stopped suddenly and laughed. "Why, look at your ol' horse!"

Here came Popeye, head up, belly rolling over that jouncing, heavy gait of his. He chested up to the board fence, whickering a low chuckle.

"He's done that ever since I turned him out," Tom said, rubbing his mouth with the back of his hand. "All he needs to hear is the dog bell and no matter where he is or what he's doin', he comes runnin' like he's tellin' me to wait up."

"Ah, Tom, he's just nib-nosin'," the guest snorted. "You think a horse misses all the work you made him do any more than you and I would miss goin' in every day?"

Tom spotted 'Lilah scrambling over the hill and pushing upwind toward a long strip of red-topped sorghum. Roberts followed her, his back to where the white horse stood watching.

"The only one I know about is Popeye," he answered testily, "and I know he liked it. You could see the way he'd study those dogs, listenin' to the whistle. Got to be where I'd give two toots to hie the dog around, and Popeye'd already be headin' in that direction, even before the dog would turn."

'Lilah was making game now, head low, her tail working like a boat propeller. Roberts shifted the open gun to his left arm.

"When I'd ground tie that horse to walk up a point, he'd usually drop his head, scroungin' something to eat. But sometimes I'd look back when the birds'd go out, and he'd have his head as high as the dogs, watchin' them outa one eye like he was watchin' us just now, like he was wondering how we'd shoot or where those birds were going."

'Lilah's orange-flecked body had gone hard two rows into the sorghum, her tail now flagging ever so slightly. Roberts motioned to his friend. "They're movin' on her some. Just step in there across her face and put 'em up."

The man looked to his gun, then egg-walked in front of the dog. When he was nearly even with 'Lilah's nose, Roberts swung around to look over the hill. Popeye was standing at the fence, ears pricked, when the covey broke and caught two quick shots...

The horse had now been down six hours. Tom tried to rouse him twice more, had sat beside the grizzled white head and talked to him, petted him, tried to help him manage a drink. Finally, he could hold off no longer: Popeye was suffering, and Roberts could not allow that. It was a matter of trust, a pact he had made with all the dogs who had shared his life, a deal he had cut with the horse, too. It was part of being fed and sheltered, worked and respected.

He walked slowly back to the farmhouse and rooted around for the phone book.

Scott Sullivan was an out-of-work coal miner who kept his family fed doing custom butchering of steers and shoats. He was a practiced hand at dispatching big animals. Roberts was still rehearsing what he wanted to say when Sullivan's voice interrupted the ringing signal. He said "hello" twice before Tom could begin talking.

It was late afternoon when Roberts watched a grimy blue pickup slowly pick its way up the rutted lane. He pulled his denim work coat from the peg by the kitchen door and ducked into the stained, brown fedora he wore to town in the winter. When Scott Sullivan pulled up in front of the barn, Tom was waiting for him.

While they shook hands, Roberts glanced over the younger man's shoulder to see the silhouette of a rifle hanging upside down in the rear window rack. "I called Todd Holt, over t' Webb's Summit," Sullivan offered. "He said he'd have his digger here after a bit. We knew you'd wanna finish with this tonight if you could."

"I 'preciate it, Scott. I'm awful sorry to have to ask you to do this. I would have done it myself, but I just…" Roberts's voice trailed off, and Sullivan looked away for a long minute while his neighbor bowed his head and dug the toe of his boot into the driveway gravel.

"Tom, you got someplace you could go for awhile? Let me and Todd take care of it for you." The sound of the backhoe rig rumbling up the county road came to both of them, and Tom could feel his belly tighten and twist like it had when Popeye had gone down that morning.

He and Sullivan spoke for a short while longer, making certain of where Holt was to work, the talk finally breaking off when the orange machine hove into view at the far boundary to Tom's farm. "Go on, now," Sullivan urged. "Todd and me can handle this. Come back in a couple hours, and it'll be done."

Suddenly, Tom Roberts was very tired. His eyes roamed the barnyard, lighting everywhere but on the paddock or out toward the approaching engine noise. Finally they came to rest on the end kennel, where Holly stood on her hind legs, front paws hooked on the chain link, tail wagging tightly against her hocks.

"I wanted to get this dog some work this morning," Tom mumbled, more to himself than to Sullivan. "She's fat as I am, sittin' around most of this season." With that, he moved away from where the blue truck was parked, walked up the hill, and disappeared into the kennel shed to fetch the bell collar. Holly was leaping up and down at her gate when he came around to get her.

They walked as fast as Roberts could manage, on past the quail pens, beyond the pond, trying to outdistance the backhoe's menacing drone. When they made the second hill beyond the house, the one overlooking most of the ground he hunted, Tom paused to get his breath, remembering all the dogs he and Popeye had followed off that knoll: Billy, the gangling setter who'd accounted for the field trial ribbons nailed up in the kennel shed; Luke, the derby who'd been killed by a prairie rattler one hot morning on the plains; Cass, a tri-color Llewellin, and stylish Elhew Trudy, Holly's mother; the tiny setter Raggs, whom Roberts couldn't break of barking when a covey went out; bloody-tailed meat dog 'Lilah, resting now in the high pasture near where Tom had directed the backhoe to dig.

He bent and belled the pointer, ordering her to "hold" while he reached inside his coat and pulled the whistle out of his shirt pocket. Two harsh blasts, and she was gone.

Roberts turned to take a long look at the empty white line of pasture fence behind the barn, then angled off in the wake of the steel bell tolling Holly's cast across the fading afternoon.

The birds were where he knew they'd be, laid up in the rough between a wide, shaggy fencerow and four rows of soybeans left by Roberts's tenant farmer. Holly was steaming back along the fence's lee side when the stop came like a sharp blow, the pointer twisted into the light breeze.

Tom let her stand until he could sleeve away the blur in both of his eyes. The quail held tight while he scuffed through the thick weeds, a wild, late-winter covey blowing out the far side of the fencerow when a single gunshot echoed over the hills.

Other titles by
COUNTRYSPORT, INC.

Dreaming the Lion: Reflections on Hunting, Fishing, and a Search for the Wild by *Thomas McIntyre*

Chasing Fish Tales: A Freewheeling Year in the Life of an Angler by *John Holt*

A. H. Fox: The Finest Gun in the World by *Michael McIntosh*

Bare November Days: A Tribute to Ruffed Grouse

Birds on the Horizon: Wingshooting Adventures Around the World by *Stuart Williams*

The Countrysport Wingshooter's Journal: A Bird Hunter's Personal Diary

Best Guns by *Michael McIntosh*

The Big-Bore Rifle: The Book of Fine Magazine & Double Rifles .375 - .700 Calibers by *Michael McIntosh*

Call of the Quail: A Tribute to the Gentleman Game Bird

Come October: Exclusively Woodcock

Eastern Upland Shooting by *Dr. Charles C. Norris*

Game Shooting: The Definitive Book on the Churchill Method of Instinctive Wingshooting and Sporting Clays by *Robert Churchill and Macdonald Hastings*

The Grand Passage: A Chronicle of North American Waterfowling

"Mr. Buck": The Autobiography of Nash Buckingham

Training Retrievers: The Cotton Pershall Method by *Bobby N. George, Jr.*

Robert Ruark's Africa by *Robert C. Ruark*

Shotgunner's Notebook: The Advice and Reflections of a Wingshooter by *Gene Hill*

The following Countrysport Press titles are also available in
DELUXE LIMITED EDITIONS:

Chasing Fish Tales: A Freewheeling Year in the Life of an Angler

Dreaming the Lion: Reflections on Hunting, Fishing, and a Search for the Wild

A Breed Apart: A Tribute to the Hunting Dogs that Own Our Souls, Volumes I & II

Bare November Days: A Tribute to Ruffed Grouse

Birds on the Horizon: Wingshooting Adventures Around the World

The Big-Bore Rifle: The Book of Fine Magazine & Double Rifles .375 – .700 Calibers

Eastern Upland Shooting

The Grand Passage: A Chronicle of North American Waterfowling

"Mr. Buck": The Autobiography of Nash Buckingham

The Countrysport limited editions feature:

- *deluxe leather binding* • *gold foil cover art*
- *gilt-edged top papers* • *commemorative title page*
- *ribbon bookmark*

For ordering information write or call:
COUNTRYSPORT
P.O. Box 1856, Traverse City, MI 49685
1-800-367-4114